DOUBLE VISION

First published in 2020 by
The Dedalus Press
13 Moyclare Road
Baldoyle
Dublin D13 K1C2
Ireland

www.**dedaluspress**.com

ISBN 9781910251683 (hardback)

Dedalus Press titles are available in Ireland
from Argosy Books (www.argosybooks.ie) and in the UK
from Inpress Books (www.inpressbooks.co.uk).

Cover design: Pat Boran

The Dedalus Press receives financial assistance from
The Arts Council / An Chomhairle Ealaíon.

DOUBLE VISION

PADDY BUSHE

DEDALUS PRESS

ACKNOWLEDGEMENTS

Primary acknowledgement must go to the artists, living and dead, well-known or anonymous, who created the sources. Is ar scáth a chéile a mhairimid. A special thank you is due to those creators whom I know personally, and who have enriched my own life, artistically and otherwise.

I wish to acknowledge a 2015 residency in Le Centre Culturel Irlandais in Paris, where this book was conceived and took its initial shape. The warm welcome and stimulation I was lucky enough to experience there was enormously encouraging. I also wish to acknowledge a 2018 Irish Writers' Centre residency in St. Mark's Church, Florence, where I was also warmly welcomed and encouraged. I am very grateful for both residencies, and I hope those who granted them are pleased with the results.

Some of these poems, or versions of them, were first published or broadcast in the following:

Cyphers, Herrings (The Aldeburgh Poetry Festival), *Irish Arts Review, Poetry Ireland Review, Southword, Sunday Miscellany* (RTÉ Radio 1), *The Irish Times, The Strokestown Anthology, The Temenos Academy Review* and *Reading the Future: New Writing from Ireland,* an anthology complied and edited by Alan Hayes to celebrate 250 years of Hodges Figgis.

Contents

BOOK ONE
PERIPHERAL VISION

I

A Vision of a Sunbeam Hung with Glasses / 17
An Abundance of Glasses / 18
Peripheral Vision / 19
Restoration / 21

II

Imogen's Wings / 25
A Moonlight Waltz / 26
Scallop / 27
Shaping Spirit / 28
The Artist Among the Mountains / 29
Thumb / 31
Piper / 33
The Piper's Exhalation / 34
The Raven's Lamentation / 35
The Hour of the Day / 36
Workshop / 37
The Art of Belief / 38
The Gilt Seahorses of Nossa Senhora del Rosario / 39
Chrysalis Smiles / 40
Raising the Siege / 41
A Poet in Bronze / 42
The Poem Rescued / 43

5

III

Statuesque / 49
The Sleep of Reason Creates Monsters / 50
During Donald Trump's Inauguration / 51
In a Walled Garden / 52
Dance of the City / 53
Badhbh / 54
Light / 55
Piobrachd / 57
The White Bear / 58
War Pipes / 59

IV

Family Meal / 63
A Postcard from Knossos / 64
Faustina Shivers / 65
Triptych for a Neighbour / 66
The Bell for Order / 69
Candle / 70
The Configuration of Love / 71
Afternoon in Olhao / 72
A Bracelet from Florence / 73

V

Afternoon Pilgrimage / 77
In a Hammock in Galicia / 79
The Place of Prayer / 80
Amergin's Ship / 81
Shaping the Place of Speech / 82
Dance / 83
The Dispute about the Immaculate Conception / 84

Pietà / 85
The Road to God Knows Where / 86
Listener / 87
Solstice / 88
Midwinter Sunset, Cill Rialaig / 89
Casting / 90
Sky Woman / 91
Woman, Moon and Mountain / 92
The Piper Abroad / 93
Forging Icarus / 94
First Day in Varnam / 95
Turning the Tune / 96

NOTES / 97

⌒

BOOK TWO
SECOND SIGHT

Cárta Poist ón Himalaya / 108
A Postcard from the Himalaya / 109
Síscéal / 110
Fairytale / 111
Nóta Cágach do Chathal / 112
A Raucous Note to Cathal / 113
Bé Ghlas d'Orsay / 114
The Green Goddess of Orsay / 115
Aonghas Úrghlas ag 70 / 118
Evergreen Aonghas at 70 / 119
Ómós do Shomhairle MacGill-Eain / 120
Homage to Sorley MacLean / 121
Sciúrd faoi Screapadal / 122
A Quick Trip into Screapadal / 123
Lagtrá / 124
Stranded / 125

An Mhuintir agus an Éigse / 126
Peoples and Poems / 127
Carraig Taibhrimh / 128
Stone Dreaming / 129
An Eachtra Nua / 130
A New Epic / 131
Cloisfead Ar Neamh / 132
I Shall Hear in Heaven / 133

II

An Manach, na Lachain agus an Loch / 136
The Monk, the Ducks and the Lake / 137
Fuaimrian / 140
Soundtrack / 141
Ag an Droichead a Cruthaíodh ar Neamh / 144
At the Bridge Made in Heaven / 145
Ag Aistriú 'Buddha in der Glorie' / 146
Translating 'Buddha in Der Glorie' / 147
Corra Bána / 148
White Egrets / 149
Scéal na gCapall / 150
A Tale of Horses / 151
Giorria Artach / 152
Arctic Hare / 153
Búireadh / 154
Bellowing / 155
Aniar Aduaidh / 156
Out of the Blue / 157
Áireamh na nDeachúna / 158
Reckoning the Tithes / 159

III

Forógra Cásca / 162
Easter Proclamation / 163
Sos Cogaidh, Nollaig 1914 / 164
Truce, Christmas 1914 / 165
Mar a Chualathas ar an nGrinneall / 166
As Was Heard on the Seabed / 167
Béasa an Bhroic / 168
Badger / 169
Gáirleog / 170
Garlic / 171
Athphósadh ar Oileán Diúra / 172
Remarriage on the Isle of Jura / 173
Geit Áthais ar Oileán Bharra / 174
Surprised by Joy on the Isle of Barra / 175
Surprised by Joy … / 176
Surprised by Joy … / 177
Marbhna Oisín / 178
Lament for Oisín / 179
Ar Chósta Malabar / 180
On the Coast of Malabar / 181
Paidir Oíche / 182
Night Prayer / 183

IV

An Logainmneoir / 186
Toponomist / 187
Coiscéim Aimhirghin / 188
The Amergin Step / 189
Freagra Scéine ar Aimhirghin / 190
Scéine's Reply to Amergin / 191
Labhrann Érannán / 192
Érannán Speaks / 193

Labhrann Donn / 196
Donn Speaks / 197
Díthreabhach, Drom Caor / 200
Hermit, Dromkeare / 201
An Géarchaoineadh, Sceilg Mhichíl / 202
The Wailing Woman, Skellig Michael / 203
Eadarlúid Oíche Gaoithe / 206
Interval on a Windy Night / 207
Oileánú / 208
Islanding / 209
Reic na Sceilge / 210
Skellig a Rock-bottom Deal / 211
Cailleach Chloiche Bhéarra / 212
The Stone Woman of Beara / 213
Ag Éisteacht Le Dord na nDamh / 216
Listening to the Roaring of the Stags / 217
Seachrán Sí / 218
A Fairy Floundering / 219
Ceangailte / 220
Harnessed / 221
Bean Chrúite na Bó / 222
Woman Milking / 223
Labhrann an Chailleach / 224
The Cailleach Speaks / 225

DEDALUS
PRESS

P
ER
IPH
ERAL
VISION
PADDY
BUSHE

H P X T Z F N

D E D A L U S

AUTHOR'S NOTE

The poems in this collection arise from my engagement as a poet with examples of various other artforms, from the prehistoric to the contemporary. Hence the title *Peripheral Vision*. I use that title to emphasise the peripherality of the poems to their sources; if they live as poems, they may not even be aware of their ancestry. Many of the sources are very well-known. Others are little-known, ephemeral and perhaps not even works of art in the conventional sense. I engaged with infinitely more works than I have written about, but the choice of what to write about was not a matter of artistic evaluation. Many of the works I contemplated moved me greatly but not into poetry. The nature of the choice remains random, mysterious — essentially a matter of a spark being ignited, or not.

I have written some very basic and fragmentary notes on the sources at the end of this book. But, to echo the collection's title, they are very peripheral to the poems. Interested readers may wish to glance at some or all of them. They are not essential.

PERIPHERAL VISION

PADDY BUSHE

DEDALUS PRESS

for Bernard O'Donoghue

I

A Vision of a Sunbeam Hung with Glasses

Right now, having for the umpteenth time
Mislaid all the glasses I have, even the pair strung
Around my neck, I remember the story of Brigid

And how she hung her dripping cloak miraculously
On a sunbeam that, shafting through her cell window,
Shone there steadfastly until the cloak was dry.

And so, looking out the window at a drizzly day —
Now even more smeared and blurred — I have
A vision: a sudden dazzlement of sunbeams

Erupting from behind the clouds, one of which —
One single lovely sunbeam — blazes an unerring path
Straight through my window, branching into slivers

So perfect for hanging glasses that you'd never miss them,
Each pair vying for attention, delightful in the floating dust.

An Abundance of Glasses

When I spilled them out on the table —
The dozen or so pairs of reading glasses
I'd got in the chain store for a throwaway
Couple of Euro a pair — I smiled and thought
I'd never again find myself searching
And muttering self-reproaches. Glinting
In cheerful yellow and pink packaging,
They winked reassurance, linked wide-open
Frames like a glittering music-hall chorus.

It was weeks afterwards that I dredged up
The image that had tugged like an undertow:
A smeared window, a cement floor, a broken
Sunbeam snagged on a heap of wire-framed
Glasses, almost all round-lensed, some broken,
Tangled like barbed wire, a *danse macabre*
Challenging onlookers to believe what they see,
Begging them never again to shut their eyes. A cello
Played in the yard outside, *adagio cantabile*.

Peripheral Vision

The way we see things is affected by what we know or what we believe.
— John Berger, *Ways of Seeing*

Given her age and where she came from, it was,
He thought, small wonder Colly started to see things
After the burial of her daughter. That was when

She forgot to ensure the dead woman's clothes
Were worn to Mass before any other wearing.
She knew she had, for good or evil, crossed a line.

Things. *Beings.* Clustered high up in corners
Where rafters had once absorbed shadows
From outside the pool of her lamplit childhood.

They were mostly kind, and meant her no harm,
She'd say. They usually came at the fall of night,
And were like a kind of company, you know,

For someone like herself who was now alone.
Moreover, they reminded her of the old days
And of the old people and the things they knew.

But sometimes, they frightened her, especially
The older one dressed in white, who combed her hair
And muttered from the ceiling, for hours on end.

She was a bad one, Colly knew, for all her *plámás*,
And they couldn't both stay in the one house.
She'd get agitated then, voice raised, eyes restless,

And once he visited to find her standing on a chair,
Flailing at the ceiling with her walking-stick,
Red and breathless with rage and imprecation.

Do you believe in the fairies, Colly? He coaxed
Her down, trying to gentle his way into her mind.
I don't believe in them, but I know they're there.

He climbed onto the chair and stretched his hand
Towards the high corner, stared into its dustiness.
There's nothing here, Colly, nothing at all to see.

Yes, but listen and I'll tell you something now,
Colly confided, as he sat earnestly across from her,
That will explain all that once you think about it.

The eye-doctor told me I had a kind of blindness
That means I see the sideways things differently.
You see, I see things that other people can't see.

He recalled his own glaucoma, the medication
He dropped each day into both eyes, to deal,
The ophthalmologist said, with peripheral blindness.

Small wonder, he mused, making his way home,
That Colly sees the things she knows are there.

Restoration

for Tim Horgan

(i)

He had entered the painting before its restoration,
Had been drawn to its headland, been buffeted
By those onshore winds hammering angular waves
Into its steely sea, heard the cacophony of seabirds

Snatching at its surface. He had felt his whole being
Stretching to the horizon, felt the occluded sun's
Enormous lightness coaxing him up to its painted
Self, its universal eye. But he had stood forlornly

In the foreground, felt the grit of the blown sand
Sting his cheeks, had narrowed his clouding eyes
And mind towards dullness. The seabirds cried
In mourning down the cold wind as he retreated

Out of the painting that, layer upon layer, had become
A place he might have been. He ached for realisation.

(ii)

After the restoration, he walked back into the painting.
And couldn't believe his eyes. He heard the same cries
Of the seabirds, felt the same sand blown by the same
Boisterous wind flinging its ragged self at the headland.

But these now were votive cries, votive incense thrown
Indiscriminately in one great raucous blaring of *I am.*
Varnishings unpeeled themselves from his amazed eyes,
As he marvelled at this fanfare of the common world.

Here and now the sun had come into its own, its own
Give and take, take and give with the sea and the clouds
That nuanced themselves from the profoundest indigo
To purest azure dancing delighted steps across the sky.

And he too was revivified, became part of the restoration,
Freshly embodied in — say it, yes, he dared — a revelation.

II

Imogen's Wings

for Imogen Stuart

In the sunlit courtyard, the great stone curves
Of those wings you sculpted take on the shine
And depth of the fresh chestnuts sprinkled

All over the grass and gravelled paths below,
And engrave the frosty air like cello-music,
A valediction forbidding mourning of the seasons.

Monumentally still, they flit constantly
Between one shape and the same other,
One for sorrow, two for joy. The space between

Those feathered slabs could encompass a globe,
Or a fallen chestnut. Their uplifted tips
Aspire like the peaks of Skellig Michael.

That white dove that flew into the Latin
Of Columbanus nestles here, gurgling warm
Approval of all this international to and fro,

Cradling it within its soft, bulging spaces.
But here too is the rush of sterner wings,
That surge of anger when you beat the air

With powerful words and swooped on those
Who dared profane that wing-haunted island.
Here are the militant wings of the Archangel.

Imogen, imagine if you will your powerful wings
Enfolding, embracing Skellig. Now the stone sings.

Centre Culturel Irlandais, Paris, October 2015

25

A Moonlight Waltz

From a great distance a poet has heard
The sad strains of its gaiety, and knows

That, like so many others, it will end
In a tristesse the creative heart knows well.

On the beach, under the moon, the dancers
Sense nothing of this. They know only

The whirl, the glide, the hum of spheres
Delighting in their every step and turn

And turnabout, rapt in an exhilaration
Of shining eyes and silver laughter, gilded

Arms and shoulders catching the light.
The musicians are shadowed by the cliff,

Apart from one whose lifted face slants
Into light, his ear cocked for every nuance,

His fingers on the fretted lute patterning
Every last thing he hears and sees.

Do not be fooled by the gaudy clothes,
The amused eyes, the knowing smile.

This one hears the echo of what is to come.
He knows the score. He'll soon strike a chord.

Scallop

These fluted curves encompass every sound
The world makes, hinged between sea and sky.
They hear those voices that will not be drowned.

Pilgrims once gathered here, praying aloud,
Holding their shells aloft to feel the bright
And radiant curves encompass every sound.

Love, too, drifted lightly ashore, and wound
Her salt-blown hair through earthly songs to tie
Herself to voices that will not be drowned.

And the lone voyagers — poor souls who found
Nor god nor love — they too sit high and dry
Where fluted shells encompass every sound.

Shingle whispers constantly, shifting its ground
To help the village brace against the tide,
Determined that its voices will not drown.

These are human shades that crowd around
Where tides ebb and flow, gods live and die.
These fluted curves encompass every sound
And hear those voices that will not be drowned.

Shaping Spirit

for Catriona O'Connor

See water at the far

        End of time wearing

Stone away with grain

        Upon grain of sand

Thrown by wave

        After wave's explosion

And yet stone never

        Wearing away

Water that shifts

        Wave after wave

Into the shape

        Of water-shaped stone

The Artist Among the Mountains

Although he had brought his pencils,
Charcoal and pastels in his rucksack

Along with his folding canvas stool
That day he trekked into the high

Mountain valley, he never felt the need
To use his sketchbook. He just unfolded

The stool, spread the tripod legs
Evenly, wedging them between clefts

Of rock and clumps of knotty heather,
And sat there the whole day. He watched

The peaks above the snowline circling him
With the curiosity of a herd, saw them

Lose their fear and settle again to ruminate.
He saw how the clouds became the snow

Around the peaks, how snow and clouds
Picked out each summit's ultimate shape,

Folding and unfolding it with infinitely
Patient attention to every changing detail.

His breathing slowed, deepened. He felt
Himself expand, felt his shoulders flex

Themselves skyward, knew the muscularity
Of rocks and ledges along his bones, the flow

Of meltwater through his veins. He realised
He was being drawn into the mountains,

Knew he was his own parchment, on which
The mountains were working. He braced

His boots like fenceposts in the rough ground
That he might let his mind climb into clouds.

Much later, descending towards the village,
He knew the mountains were already painted.

Thumb

for Maura Dooley

(i)

The dedication? The truth is I mixed up sculptors
At the Pompidou Centre, where a ten-metre

Golden thumb dominated the square outside,
Backgrounded by a hoarding for a Jim Dine exhibition,

And I assumed *Thumb* was his and then I thought
Of your 'Cleaning Jim Dine's Heart', and I thought

Of a possible companion piece, so here I am —
Serendipitously mistaken — offering this poem to you.

(ii)

Here, then: César's *Thumb*. He must have smiled
At that echo of absolute power of life and death.

Yet so much life rests in this raised insouciance
That, like your *Heart*, has everything in it. So like

All other thumbs and yet so much itself, its whorled
Thumbprint a singular universal, an irreproducible

Intricacy that repeats *we are* as it repeats *I am*,
Holding itself stubbornly up against all good reason.

31

This *Thumb*, like *Heart*, has room for everything.
Sucking wisdom into itself, it becomes oracular,

Inclining its cowled head towards passers by,
A thumbnail like the pattern of all countenance,

A head bowed now and again in acquiescence,
Above all, bowed in constant acknowledgement.

Piper

for Bob Ó Cathail

Quietly, then, the piper begins. Settled in his chair,
He elbows the bellows, coaxing long sighs
While searching for tunings in resonant air.

He pipes up a rooster who raucously declares
Daybreak at midnight with all its hues and cries,
But doesn't stir himself, rests easy in the chair.

He pipes up a fox-chase, pipes the running hare
And pipes the thrush who pipes the reasons why
Love's grace-notes travel wide, glittering in the air.

Now he pipes the howl of women in despair
Where torn, bloody flags and broken bodies lie.
The piper makes no move, rooted in the chair.

A nimbus of afterlight settles like a prayer
As old notes linger when a tune has gone by
And passed upward into high, remote air.

His head's thrown back. Light ripples through his hair.
The earth exhales in drones, the chanter scales the sky.
Although the piper barely stirs, rooted in the chair,
He travels deep and wide, layering tremulous air.

The Piper's Exhalation

for Carlos Núñez

Because his whole heart
And soul overflowed

With the air that inspired him,
And because his *gaita* likewise

Had inhaled almost to bursting
The music of what happens,

The piper snatched a moment
From his throbbing mouthpiece

To exhale into the gobsmacked air
An ululation resounding somewhere

Between a howl and a whoop
Of exultation over Galicia.

The Raven's Lamentation

His croaking aches for *portaireacht,* for the bubbling
Of shorebirds, for the dance tunes of thrush and ouzel

Invisibly silvering the air from among the branches,
For larksong losing the run of itself in tumbling skies.

The raven notes all this, craves all this, but knows
It will not be his. He grieves that only the drones

Answer him, grieves that no piped note will ever jig
Or reel him to enchantment. Only villages mourning

Their battle-dead, only a howling against famine
Or against the old malice of the sea will summon

The harsh inevitability of his music. Over and over
He mourns his solitary way down the stony wind.

The Hour of the Day

He feels the floor tilt, tipping him towards
A different plane as soon as he draws

The bow smoothly across incredulous strings
That are beside themselves with excitement.

Even his feet lose the run of themselves, slide
Down from under him. No matter, he is pure

Spirit, his music drawing him up and out
Of himself, of the room and into the clouds,

Where he stays for the length of a few tunes,
As he does, at this hour, every morning.

Workshop

So this is where the whole things starts:
With rasp, vice, anvil, pincers, chisel,
All these instruments for soaring. Here

Is what polishes marble to smooth passage
Across immeasurable skies, burnishes vast
Distances in brass, measures the depth

Of a kiss in stone, of an infant's dreams.
Here is celestial toil: bird, pillar and orb,
To be hammered and tonged, hoisted

And pulleyed up and over themselves
Into space, into shapes beyond weight,
Beyond recognition, discovering shapes

Beyond instruments. And to return to be
Worked on again. The whole thing again.

The Art of Belief

But sometimes the artist will lead you
And your amazed eyes where reason

Absolutely refuses to go. A painted saint, say,
His long, bony fingers — a piper's, maybe —

Joined so delicately just at their very tips,
Arched and opened around a universe,

Are buttressing what you will not believe,
Making vaulted certainty of the air between,

As if a great bronze door has been opened
To reveal the very entrails of conviction.

And the air, being spun of filigreed gold
All around him, sings notes you know

You cannot hear. But still you see them
Embodied here, tangible beyond belief.

The Gilt Seahorses of Nossa Senhora del Rosario

for Melissa Newman

The altar bulged with baroque *buaileam sciath,*
Resplendent with rococo razzmatazz,
Glorious with the gilt of its grandeur!
Here was *mór is fiú* and braggadocio,
Here the weighty worthiness of a world
Dazzled by itself! And dazed. And drained.
Casting his eyes to the ground, Jesus wept.

Until from under bent brows, to left and right,
Halfway up each ponderous framing column,
He made out two curling seahorses,
Who each flicked a gilt, translucent tail,
Rested its long equine jaw on a ledge
And sent him messages in speech bubbles.
Lifting his eyes to heaven, Jesus winked.

Chrysalis Smiles

for Darragh Morgan and Siripong Albert Tiptan

And it was just then, just at the very moment
The music had climbed almost to overreaching,

But had steadied in time into perfect pitch
Like a roped climber upright on a sharp ridge,

That the two violinists smiled at one another
Momentarily across continents. Their smiles,

Wriggling themselves up and out through arched
And concentrated brows, thrummed and spiralled

Upwards like a pair of butterflies in a Chinese story
To settle in chandeliered splendour overhead.

From where they beamed down on the quintet,
On the amazed violas daring themselves to follow,

On the cello sawing through its melancholy depths,
On the piano, lightening itself, preparing for flight.

Raising the Siege

Wearily I raise my staff, invoking ancient arts
Against the wolves who howl outside the walls
Through this long, brutal siege of the heart.

Iron bands squeeze tighter, the city starves.
The air is frozen with omens of downfall.
Fearful, I clutch my staff, uncertain of my art.

We walk the city, a place now utterly apart.
Windows reflect only ourselves, appalled
At this implacable siege of the heart.

Shadows outside swell, begin to be heard
As chain-linked rhythm, as sinister footfall
Growing loud, denouncing the staff of art.

The spirit freezes. Our own souls grow hard.
The inevitable claws at us, as time crawls
Along besieged passageways of the heart.

And still we cry out for a blaze against the dark
In full knowledge of the final, ineluctable fall.
Resolved, I lift our staff, invoking all my art
To raise once more the endless siege of the heart.

A Poet in Bronze

He's statued outside the house
Where he was born and grew up
Spellbound by nearby church bells.

But the poet's face, like all the faces
He ever had, or pretended to have,
Is hidden by a huge, bronze book

Bearing just two words, engraved
One to the front, one to the back:
The city's name, the poet's name.

I laugh, reminded again of my father
Remonstrating with me: *why must*
Your nose be forever stuck in a book?

The Poem Rescued

I

The clergy wanted to own the poem:
The where and when, the how
And why of it. The whole of it.

They insisted its provenance must
Be ordained, its utterance mediated
And sanctioned by the initiated.

They didn't want the sunlight
To gild it, nor to find its shadows;
Didn't want it to hear the traffic.

They didn't want any passers-by
To stare, thinking they recognised
A neighbour, or a long-lost friend.

They were adamant the poem
Needed shelter, needed above all
Not to have notions about itself.

So they raised it high into a niche
Among the other statued poems
That lined the cathedral's walls.

The poem's slow tears welled
Into stone, calcified into a narrative
Priests would decode for pilgrims.

II

Unauthorised, but with a forged
Name-card hanging around its neck,
A song slipped in with the pilgrims,

And went down secretly to the crypt,
Where it disembodied itself
Into invisibility, and hid the name-card.

Quietly the song began to hum itself
Under its breath, for the time being
Audible only to the surrounding dead.

Then, still all the while invisible,
It made its way back up to the nave
Step by step beginning to be heard,

Amplifying its multiple voices
Until it filled the great cathedral
Silencing the voices of the priests.

Magnifying itself along the soaring
Stained glass windows, it scaled
Pillars and vaulting arches, and pulled

Itself into the huge bronze cupola,
A breathing space for its dizzy self
And for the tiny searching faces,

Awestruck and infinitely far below.
They heard it resonate in the dome,
Heard it surpass its words and music,

Heard it become planetary ripples,
Infinite. Unseen, the song descended
And, taking the poem by the hand,

Walked unhindered down the aisle,
Unlocked the bronze doors and led
The way out into the sunlit square.

Here they strolled, found a café, dallied
Over coffee on the terrace, smiling
At passers-by who sometimes smiled back.

III

Statuesque

for Laurence Edwards

The man bends under the weight of the cuttings
He will draw home. He has spent the day hewing
The small branches and shoots permitted him.

The leaves and twigs will feed the cow. She is tethered
Because he owns no grazing. The branches will keep
The fire smouldering. We will manage, he thinks.

His load is tied with pieces of thin rope,
Tightened beyond all measure. The pack grows
Dense, its branches scored by the rope's pressure.

When he heaves it onto his shoulders, sinews
And branches knot into each other, the man grows
Into his load, his load an impetus to raise him up

In silhouette against the light. You might imagine him
Heroic, bronzed. Imagine something noble in all this.

The Sleep of Reason Creates Monsters

Prophecy's black candles cast a deep shadow.
Monsters are rumoured, name by whispered name.
Reason has slept and is waking to madness.

Succession now falls on the fool and the gambler,
Jokers and knaves have trumped the royal game.
Prophecy's black candles cast a deep shadow.

The play's at the bidding of bankers and barons
Whose winnings are counted below the dark flames.
Reason has slept and is waking to madness.

If drilling or poison make the rich land barren
The people are schooled and will know who to blame.
The ones who are Other inhabit deep shadows.

Those who dissent should know what will happen:
The managed confessions in the public squares
Where Reason still sleeps, but will waken to madness.

If the tower cannot reap, the tower then will harrow.
In the cellars are ledgers and instruments of shame.
Prophecy's black candles have cast a deep shadow
Where Reason once slept. We have woken to madness.

Wednesday, November 9th 2016

During Donald Trump's Inauguration

I closed my eyes, to conjure from the 1950s
An image of that towering man Paul Robeson
Singing his heart and soul across the border

Between Washington State and Canada,
When tides of race and power and wealth
Surged all as one to try to drown him out,

Snatching his passport lest his songs be heard
By the Mine, Mill and Smelter Workers Union.
I conjured the noisy flatback truck manoeuvred

To the border, and the straining loudspeakers
Bearing the burden of his songs where his masters
Feared to grant him passage. And I conjured

All those gathered thousands rising to *Joe Hill*,
To *Ol' Man River* and to *Let My People Go,* rising
To anthems that might crack dividing walls.

And this still I hoard: that profound voice rolling
Across the barriers built by poisoned money,
Urgent with the wish to make America good.

In a Walled Garden

There are street noises. Church bells overhead
Reassure me. Things being normal as they seem,
I cannot believe what is now being said.

Officials have warned against being misled
Into outdated loyalties, to beware of extreme
Threats in our streets to the church bells overhead.

People have disappeared. Officials say they've fled —
Clear evidence of a plot against the regime.
It's hard to believe what I sometimes hear said.

At night, sirens. They fill the air with dread,
Then urgent steps, warnings. Sometimes a scream
Muffled by street noise, church bells overhead.

Outside my wall's barred window, sullen as lead,
The river crawls by, inexorably. Downstream,
The sewers overflow with what's being said.

But here there is calm, order. A wall, a hedge,
Shelter me. In the sunlight, I can sit and dream
Of ordinary street noise, church bells overhead.
I must not begin to believe what's being said.

Dance of the City

On walls, under arches, the whole city chants
An anthem that swells and sways through the crowd.
Here are many as one in one swirling dance.

The winter's been long. The palace remains harsh.
But the dance in the streets has emptied each house
And on walls, under arches, the whole city chants.

By churches and markets the dancers advance
And retreat, high-steppingly proud
Of being many as one in one swirling dance.

The pulse of the dancing is lifting those hearts
That were wounded, those heads that were bowed.
On walls, under arches, the whole city chants

Then one who is breathless is all at once grasped
And linked and uplifted, spun and spun around
By the song of the many into one swirling dance.

The courtiers in the palace are watching aghast,
Watching the dancers, hearing songs sung out loud
On walls, under arches. The whole city chants
Of the many as one in this one swirling dance.

Badhbh

The raven and the carrion crow raise hooded heads,
Beaks bloodied from the tearing, to croak gratitude,

Salutations to their goddess sister, who has once more
Scattered rich pickings. The spread of severed limbs,

They know, is an earnest of so much more to come.
She gallops high above the carnage, her black horse

Fragmenting the sky, her cry a triumphant howling
Of sirens. She always carries the day, no matter

Who claims victory, or the right to victory. Today
The city's theatres and cafés bleed. Tomorrow

Frontier villages will crumple, will be hung with votive
Images of the city's dead. She will ride a white horse.

Light

(i)

A single light serves many purposes. The same
Lantern that clarifies the confusion in the square,

And allows the execution squads to do their work,
Shines too on the final defiance of the partisans,

Allows their people to remember how they died,
Eyes gleaming, fists raised, allows their last words

To hang as an illuminated banner in the anthemic air,
A banner to light the many dark gatherings to come.

(ii)

There is too the light gleaming from attics and cellars
Where gatherings whisper accounts of the newly dead

And, under bare bulbs that light dusty corners, create
A manifesto to spread its light in circles that widen

To encompass the earth. This is the light that will guide
The men at screens who will guide the men with bombs,

And the screens themselves will light in silent celebration
Of attics and cellars darkened, of screams never heard.

(iii)

This is not to say that the execution squads see light
In the way the partisan sees it, nor that the torturer

Knows light with the same clarity as his spotlit victim.
This is not to say the king believes in the burning cross

He ignites for his people to flock towards, nor is this
To deny those heroes who, dazzled, die by the light.

It is just to plead for a light less endless, less relentless.
It is to say that pure light burns eyes from their sockets.

Piobrachd

for David Power

Dark women wail in the midst of the slaughter,
As though the earth itself exhaled suffering, sounds
Never before known, never to be known hereafter.

Here's feral lamentation. Drones howl down chanter
Until the ground plays itself like an open wound
And dark women wail in the midst of the slaughter.

They have heard old keenings, fragments of folklore
Preserved by elders, but have never before howled
Such a savage harrowing. Nor will they do hereafter.

The rites will come later, the sprinkling of water.
There will be processions and the raising of mounds.
Now dark women wail in the midst of the slaughter.

Here are the fields and the ruins they fought for,
The meeting hall, the place of worship. They vow,
Having wailed so fiercely, never to wail hereafter.

And still there are anthems. Still sons and daughters
Sing words of old anthems not yet drowned out
By dark women wailing in the midst of the slaughter.
Still the anthems are taught. And will be sung hereafter.

The White Bear

The great rolling hindquarters are urgent
With momentum. He is charged with the need
To make good the season, to hunt in lucent
Monochromes of sky and ice and water,
To bloody the lunging paws, and then to sleep
In darkness comforted by memories of light.

But he hesitates, reluctant forepaws digging in
Against the unexpected tilt of the floe.
His raised head moves slowly, like a scanner.
He hears the bellowing of many glaciers
Calving out of their time, gets a warm smell
He doesn't yet know. Knows it must be feared.

War Pipes

A piper long astray
In the Cave of Gold
And in his wits
For generations
Past and to come
Playing night and day
Maddened into prayer
For one thing only
A third hand he craved
That might grasp a sword.

IV

Family Meal

Again, the same dream. He's outside
The window of his own house.
Again he has locked himself out.

There is a table, pooled in light.
There is a family, an evening meal.
There is a woman, a boy, a girl

Facing the silhouette of a man
Whose unlit back is to the window.
The girl stares towards both men,

Sees only the man in the room. The man
Outside does not recognise the dark
Bulk of the man the girl watches

In the lamplight. Nor can he hear
Anything she says across the table
Or any answer the man may make.

The rigid smile she hides behind
Shows nothing of the icy shards
He feels encircle her heart and eyes.

He knows it well now, this dream
Where he has locked himself outside.
Years and years too late he beats

At window glass that will not shatter
But echoes dully like hammered
Lead weights around his guilty heart.

A Postcard from Knossos

for Pat Boran

Dedalus, on the other hand, always knew
Exactly what he was doing, being wary
Of high flyers, of the big splash, of playing
To the gods. He liked to push simple things —
A cow-hide, feathers, wax, a ball of string —
Right to their limits in great undertakings,
In labyrinths of death, in tracing the intricacies
Of love's secret passages, but not beyond.

Here, where it all started, he's known still
As a down-to-earth man. Extraordinarily so.

Faustina Shivers

She knows no shame for that
Formed part of the bargain
When she sold her soul
Just a normal transaction
It cannot be called diabolical
She tells her everyday self
A corporate takeover of a soul
Regularly she checks the locks
On visions outside of contract
And wanders abandoned rooms
A shiver in endless search
Of a backbone to land on

Triptych for a Neighbour

in memoriam Eddie Falvey

(i) EARLY POTATOES

This spring, again, I remember how every year,
The first fine February day that came, he'd say
It's a bit soon, but God knows maybe I might
Throw down a *dorn* of earlies in the morning.

To imagine a gauntlet being thrown down
Is fanciful, I know. But as I sort this year's
Sprouted seed, he's again over my shoulder,
And he's once more shaking his fist at winter.

(ii) LANDING

I remember too the day he swore his wits
Were gone astray, with the fright he'd got
From my garden Buddha he'd seen silhouetted
On the cliff, meditating on the conjunction
Of sea and land and sky. He had glanced up
Just as he landed, right on a top-tide swell,
After a spin out with the lads. Never before,
He said, did it loom over him quite like that.

I seldom go to sea myself now, just an odd spin
In the kayak around Carraig Éanna and its seals,
Avoiding the reefs he'd shown me. Hauling pots
In a hard wind is just a memory. But I still know
To keep my bow into the swell, to watch for
The backwash off the rock, for a north-westerly
Rising on hot afternoons. Above all, he warns,
You must keep your wits about you on the sea.

(iii) EARLY MAY GALE

Today, the fifteenth of the month, the early May
Gale he foresaw every year is blowing itself out,
Shaking the white blossoms just starting to come
On what promises to be a good crop of earlies,

If, as it should, the gale settles with the sea. Buddha,
I am sure, senses the lovely foliage over his shoulder,
But contemplates only the sea, as if to keep all our keels
Even, our wits about us, on sea, on land, in all seasons.

The Bell for Order

i.m. Eamon Langford

You always sang that the October *wind*
(to rhyme with *kind)* sang around
The Castle of Dromore. It suited you,
The old-fashioned correctness, the urge

To do the right thing. And so you did
In the Corner House, tinkling the little bell
For good order for all the performers,
Each one in their own time and space.

Such a sweet passing bell! The sea-swell
That seized your heart next day in Kells
Was just a ripple, a tinkle, but enough
To call for order, gently. It suited you.

Now there's the ordinary sound of wind
Around Iveragh, lamenting one of a kind.

Candle

Afterwards he
Circled his arms
Around her
Joined his hands
As if in prayer
Bowed his head
To the incense
Of her
Spread hair
Flickered
Asleep awake
Intense
Alpha
Incandescent
Omega
A candle
Awaiting everyday
Resurrection
Ascending
Into flame.

The Configuration of Love

We made love the night you turned sixty-nine.
No, not that playful configuration of the young,

But configured still, and still configuring
Trajectories that veer now and again

Towards infinity, on axes of time, of space.
And as we drift, elliptically into sleep

Trajectories dissolve, axes dissolve,
Become random, serendipitous. Like stars.

Afternoon in Olhao

When, after love, the celebratory sun
Slants through the shutters on me

Clinging into your curved back
With my face in your tousled hair,

I nuzzle into the memory of half
A century ago, your uniformed

Back curved into me as I crossbar
You back to school, daring to lean

Into the curve, daring to inhale
Such lifetimes, such fragrances!

A Bracelet from Florence

Crossing the *Ponte Vecchio* that spans
The narrowest point of the Arno below,
I brooded again on that capricious throw
Of the dice that upended all our plans
For you to join me here. One untied lace
Was all it took, one awful breathless fall
To clarify our fragility, and clarify all
That sunders us, and sunders place from place.

Enough of that. A nameless bridge in Cork
Being where you broke your wrist, I thought
Of *caol*, of span, of the hurt hand I long
To kiss. So in a jewellery shop I picked
A token of so much we both have missed,
And bring this silver bracelet for your wrist.

*"caol" in Irish means both "wrist" and "narrow",
sometimes specifically the narrow part of a river.*

Afternoon Pilgrimage

for Antonio Raúl de Toro Santos

Because it had been said we must visit
Santo André de Teixido while we live,
Or else be spirited there later as toads

Or lizards, we set off down the steep path
Marked by votive cairns and stitched tightly
Into tumbled granite by sea-pink and crocus,

Clambering down ladders of heat and light
And along a path beaten through yew trees
Whose shadowing gave the village its name.

Mica and quartzite flashed here and there
Among the boulders, whispering insistently
About that otherworld long since denied.

The path steadily dipped and dropped
Along abrupt zigzags that turned back
On themselves like an endless argument,

Down to orange tiles, stone walls and narrow
Twisting lanes pungent with dung and straw,
Then the village, the fountain, the church

Pied with slated stone and gleaming mortar,
Overflowing with candlelight and painted
Breadcrumb statues hawked in the square.

And as we left, past the parking area jammed
With buses, and along the double yellow lines
Of the new access road, it was hard to make out

Which way we had come down, which world
We had entered or left or which way back up
Would lead to wherever it was we'd been going.

In a Hammock in Galicia

for José Miguel Giraldez

Moulded into a net hammock
     Moored between two trees
In an orchard sloping south,

     The light through a mesh of leaves
Stippling dewdropped windfalls.
     And somewhere, children playing,

I think of the Milesians
     Who, they say, left these parts
To settle on Ireland's west coast,

     And of Amergin, who claimed
He was wind and wave and weather,
     Sun and moon and stars.

I laugh, not quite out loud.
     The hammock sways, just a little.
Nearby, a peach drops into silence.

The Place of Prayer

The afternoon light in this place of prayer
Is luminous with honey and amber. The place

Could be outdoors, a forest of birch, say,
In late October. Or it could be sunlight

Shafting through stained glass, pinpointing
Dust motes pendant in air that's tremulous

With long waiting for something to happen,
Or mourning something which already has.

There is, insistent but still in the background,
The heavy rhythm of slow, painstaking trains.

Here the visible shrinks, becomes the audible,
Becomes the utterance of the unsayable.

Light and texture, even the faint smell of ashes,
Are a susurration of words woven into prayer,

The warp and weft of which now rise and fall
Into patterns that are pure sound, moanings

Of disbelief that repeat themselves over
And over until they whisper, barely, *we believe.*

Amergin's Ship

for Holger Lönze

Because he wanted simply to be as one
With the swelling wave and the wind,

With the salmon and with the stars
Clustered in the eye of the gannet,

He sailed north when the four winds
Blossomed together in a compass,

North being the petal that trembled
Towards the grey ambiguous headlands

The elder swore he scried from the tower
Infinitely far beyond the salty horizon.

The ship's skin-lined planking breathed
Brine and wind, welded gust and swell

In a coupling that surpassed navigation.
Sea and ship hammered one another

Into one another's shape, shaped
Wind and weather to the poet's will

To be the voyage, to be the landfall
And the words that marked the landfall,

To be the land and the land's creatures
To be the stones raised in commemoration,

To be the ship beached forever on the land,
And the words singing themselves into bronze.

Shaping the Place of Speech

for John Carey

Absorbing soft vowels
From the formless air

> From the exhalations
> Of river, lake and sea;

Enclosed by the consonants
Of summits, shores and ridges

> That stretch towards horizons
> Veering between planes;

Punctuated by raised stones
That yearn for articulacy,

> Yearn to be monuments
> Set far down and firm;

Conjured again and again
By the poet's incantations,

> The place becomes landscape
> Shaped to its own utterance.

Dance

for Karen Hendy

At first your dance steps are slow.
Slow. Slow as the black bog's
Ooze and seep swallowing
Leaf and branch, root and bole,
Whispering ineluctable decay.

A bubbling, then, in the dark.
Tentative. And slow. Tentative,
Tentative, tentative and then pat
-terns appear and disappear and
Then tapping and tapping and tap.

And the oakwood echoing, echoing
To the patterned blows of axe upon
Axe for charcoal, for smelting, for iron
In the soul, and blitzkrieg advance and
Advance and advance on the land.

Retreat now, into the blackbird's sweet
Song on the blossoming briar. Ease
Your heart into airiness, your steps
Into stars patterning the sky, hands
Bridging all gaps. All abask. All aglow.

The Dispute about the Immaculate Conception

The woman around whom the dispute
Is centred, is herself outside the circle,

As of now above it. She throws her eyes
To Heaven. Whether her eyes,

Her outstretched arms casting aside
The dark cloak from her scarlet robe

Are submissive or despairing or just
Exasperated, she is not in a position

To tell us. All the words are below,
Being rolled out on scrolls by cherubs

Or pointed at by distinguished men,
Their mitres and books held by boys

Who are bored now but will learn.
Just one young scholar is doubtful,

Raises a questioning eye towards her.
But he does not disturb the dispute

Which circles around words, such as
Concupiscence, virginity, conception.

Below the circle of disputation, two
Naked lovers lie sleeping, satisfied.

When the circle turns, as it now
And again will do, they will be above.

Pietà

Christ lay stretched, broken yet heroic
In his mother's arms, she exaltedly
In mourning, her soul now magnified

As she held that embodied sacrifice
Close to her, laying it open also
To receive the world's homage.

The broken body of a man, the robed
Woman in mourning. The old pattern
Becoming a pattern for a new order.

Jesus retched. Wounded Jesus refused
That which had been ordained, refused
The burial, the tomb, the heroic repetition.

Reaching up, he wiped his mother's face
Clear of its exaltation, its magnificent grief,
Of all but the comfort and grief that must be.

Androgynously, then, he arose and cradled her,
Became his mother comforting her infant self,
Refusing that which was eternally ordained.

And this was the true, and will be the everlasting
Resurrection of Christ, the consolation of his mother.

The Road to God Knows Where

for Seán Hardie

Especially when a milky sky and a pale
Dusty road that had ranged the valley
Has dissolved itself in that white opacity;

Especially when this gleaming fluency
Separates itself, and a rolling fog sours
What is left of the day; then the long road

To God knows where snakes back on itself,
Sloughing off all knowledge, and all at once
Nowhere is there any road, and God is nowhere.

Listener

If you would listen well, and truly hear
Rumours from below the clay, leave space
Between the cupped hand and the waiting ear,

And listen to the deep earth. All of the dear
Dead are still singing, or whispering prayers
That you may listen, and may truly hear.

Grant all of them entrance, grant them clear
Passage in their own time, at their own pace,
Between the cupped hand and the listening ear.

Let long lost rivers break the surface here
Funnelling themselves into a sunlit race
That you can listen to, and truly hear.

Let children play here, play without fear
And jubilantly make it their own place
Between the cupped hand and the listening ear.

The faintest, furthest sound will be as near
As starlight silvering your upturned face
If you have listened well, and cherish what you hear
Between the cupped hand and the enlightened ear.

Solstice

Dubhluachair. Thin rush-light just
Enough to huddle around a word
That bears such a weight of darkness.

Black rushes. Dark light of the year
Whose turning is fearfully hoped for.
The dark of this stone row marks

The sun's deepest down descent
Behind the mountain horizon distant
Beyond any measure that we know,

Who know only to gather around hope
And hold close our circled rush-lights
Finding little spurts of warmth in words.

Íochtar Cua, 21 December 2017

Midwinter Sunset, Cill Rialaig

for Tomás Ó Carragáin

Outside, all day, a low
Dull begrudging light.
In the abbot's cell, our own dark
Cradles us, cradles
Our fearful selves locked
Together for the year's dying, praying
For fusion, for rebirth,
Willing our selves into one,
Into oneness with the One's earth.

Now the old light falters through
This slabbed passageway
Whose orientation we calculated
Into our sacred masonry.
We have built a tenebrous shelter
Of stones that are the bones of light.
We have listened to the stone. Now see
The light assert its way along the slabs,
Refracted once more to its true course.

Casting

Here, then, is beginning. Cowhide bellows
Settle into themselves, into rhythm.
Their rasping is the earth whispering

Its own deepest secrets to the furnace
Scooped into the ground, the caked walls
Shaped with fireclay, bound with dung.

Smoke- blackened faces now and again
Catch firelight, anxious eyes reflecting
A covenant against encroaching darkness.

A murmuring, a sudden urgent movement
Scatters a constellation of sparks.
The charcoal glows almost unbearably

And the crucible changes colour, throbs
Like a sea buffeted by a thunderstorm.
Someone tongs the crucible, holds it

A sacred moment, then pours a practised
Stream of molten ore to fill the mould.
There is a low ripple of approval, of relief.

Here, now, are bells to initiate ceremonies
And sound belief. Here are metal harpstrings
Drawn meticulously towards a fine sweetness.

And, raising its great curved head like a swan,
A bronze trumpet exhales the song of the earth
Proclaiming the moment of its eternal beginning.

Sky Woman

for Aya Takagi

She walks the sky, and combs the clouds for stars
Where there are none, because she's always yearned
For things that lie behind the things that are.

She loves to feel the earth, to walk the paths
Her people walk. But she was also born
To walk the sky and comb the clouds for stars.

A harebell's chime, a rowan's sudden flare,
She reads as signals that it's time to turn
Towards paths that lie beneath the paths that are.

The villagers have mapped the paths that mark
The routes for trade. Now only she discerns
The skyward paths that comb the clouds for stars.

She knows by heart the heavy laws they've carved
Deep into stone slabs. But she has also learned
The law that came before the laws that are.

And secretly she hoards an ancient shard
Of law inscribed upon a shattered urn:
Go walk the sky, go comb the clouds for stars,
And seek what lies beyond the things that are.

Woman, Moon and Mountain

for Lisbeth Mulcahy

There is a moon
Edged clean with frost
Rising in an indigo sky.

There is a mountain
Deep and dark-shadowed
Below silvered layers.

There is a woman
Crimson with the burden
Of the world's blood.

The woman, with all the strength
Of her outstretched limbs, yearns
For the moon and for the illumination
Of the moon's embrace. She howls,

Wordlessly, as once more the moon
Rises in heedless, bloodless splendour.
She retreats, once more, to the shelter
She has fashioned from the darkness.

The Piper Abroad

In the end he wanted to go home
To the island where salt winds,

In from the great ocean, droned
The winter long, until returning

Seabirds chanted exuberantly
Of migration as they nested.

He wanted it all, wanted the whole
Being there and not being there,

The leaving and the coming back,
Language and the loss of language,

The forgotten songs and their safe
Refuge in collectors' manuscripts.

He yearned for the island's cradle,
Yearned for its grave. And, yearning,

He played the lovely, fragmented
Uncertainties of the migrant heart.

Forging Icarus

... it was not an important failure. — W.H. Auden

In the end, then, is this — whatever importance
Or lack of it is attached — a simple failure?

To have gone towards and undergone
Such downright euphoria that height

And sea and sun were all the one
Wonderful tempering, to have been

Forged and fragmented and beaten
Whole in such fusion and fission

Of light that every last scrap of him
Was hammered into that great disc,

Still to reverberate day after perfect
Brazen day: is this no more than failure,

Important or otherwise? Now and again
The ploughman raises unhappy eyes

From his furrow, the shipping merchant
From his accounts, and they yearn.

First Day in Varnam

for Beena K.J.

And yes, believe it or not, below the veranda
Where our clothes, rinsed of travel dust,

Hang gratefully in the sunlight, there really is
Shaded by a great fig tree, a lotus pond

With frogs pulsing out something important
I do not understand. And I understood

Only here and there the wisdom a *bean feasa*
This morning rooted and plucked from the air

And clay and leaves. So much I do not grasp
Either here or there. But I have begun to see,

Opaquely, that here is something divinely
Of the earth, something earthily of the divine.

bean feasa: Gaelic for a wise woman with knowledge of herbal cures

Turning the Tune

for Steve Cooney

Sweet antipodean, you turn the globe of music
Upside down, sprinkling abundant grace notes
As your fresh footprints trace old songlines.

When you close those absorbent eyes, your guitar
Tightens itself into the strings of a blind harper
Whose music offers its hand across centuries.

Da mihi manum. Give me your hand. And now
Hemispheres spin into the mirrors of themselves,
Their tunes and turnings handed on, handed down

The long meridians of memory, across the latitudes
Of kinship. Here is where we choose our equator,
And align the axis on which our world will spin.

Tabhair dom do lámh. Here's a universe of hands
Turning tunes. *Uni versus.* Towards the one turning.

NOTES
(with reservations)

These notes about specific sources for the poems are offered as background material that may be of interest to some readers. I include them with some reservations, not least a hesitation to impose them on those sources. The poems are not intended to be *about* the various sources that partly gave rise to them. Indeed, in many cases they deal with concerns and insights that are very different from those of the sources. I intend the poems to stand or fall on their own. If they do not work independently of their sources, they cannot be seen to succeed as poems. I will be quite happy for readers not to consult these notes.

I

Peripheral Vision My own thoughts about how we experience and appropriate artistic work, as well as various personal experiences, were brought into focus when reading John Berger's book, a sentence from which is quoted as an epigraph.

A Vision of a Sunbeam Hung with Glasses The story of Brigid's cloak hanging miraculously on a sunbeam is found in the 7th century *Life of Saint Brigid* by Cogitosus.

An Abundance of Glasses The image referred to is a photograph by the Polish photographer Stanislaw Mucha taken after the Auschwitz-Birkenau concentration camp was liberated.

Restoration The painting referred to is *The Monk by the Sea* by Caspar David Friedrich, which was restored in 2015 (Alte Nationalgalerie, Berlin). The immediate context of the poem was my having cataracts removed.

II

Imogen's Wings Refers to Imogen Stuart's sculpture *The Flame of Human Dignity*, in the courtyard of the Centre Culturel Irlandais, Paris.

A Moonlight Waltz Suggested by two paintings *Summer Night* by Winslow Homer in the Musée d'Orsay, Paris and *The Lute Player* by Frans Hals in the Louvre, Paris. In the background also was the poem *Sad Strains of a Gay Waltz* by Wallace Stevens and the musical piece *Valse Triste* by Jean Sibelius.

Scallop Maggie Hambling's sculpture *Scallop* celebrates the composer Benjamin Britten and stands on the beach at Aldeburgh, Suffolk. The words "I hear those voices that will not be drowned", a line from Britten's opera Peter Grimes, are cut through the metal of the sculpture.

Shaping Spirit A response to a number of water-and-stone themed paintings by Catriona O'Connor which formed part of an exhibition of her work at St. John's Art Centre in Listowel in April 2019.

The Artist Among the Mountains Suggested by the painting *A Portrait of Ambrogio Raffaele* by John Singer Sargent (Palazzo Pitti, Florence).

Thumb The sources are specified in the poem.

Piper Suggested by a painting by Bob Ó Cathail.

The Piper's Exhalation Written in response to various pieces played by the Galician piper Carlos Nuñez

The Raven's Lamentation Suggested by the old Scottish Gaelic song *Pìobrachd Dhòmhnuill Dhuibh.*

The Hour of the Day Suggested by the painting *Violinist at the Window* by Henri Matisse (Centre Pompidou, Paris).

Workshop The reference behind the poem is *L'Atelier Brancusi,* the gallery recreating the workshop of the sculptor Constantin Brancusi (Centre Pompidou, Paris).

The Art of Belief Suggested by the painting *Saint Dominic* by Cosimo Tura (Uffizi Gallery, Florence).

The Gilt Seahorses of *Nossa Senhora del Rosario* The church in question is in Olhao, Portugal.

Chrysalis Smiles Written after a recital presented as part of the Valentia Chamber Music Festival in August 2018.

Raising the Siege Suggested by an RTÉ National Symphony

Orchestra performance of Shostakovich's *Leningrad Symphony*, conducted by Stanislav Kochanovsky, in the National Concert Hall in October 2018.

A Poet in Bronze Written in a café beside a sculpture entitled *Homage to Pessoa* by Jean-Michel Folon in Largo de São Carlos, Lisbon.

The Poem Rescued Suggested by a recording of Gregorio Allegri's *Miserere*, as sung by the Choir of King's College, Cambridge, on the CD *The Renaissance of Italian Music*.

III

Statuesque Written in response to a bronze sculpture by Laurence Edwards at The White House Farm, Great Glemham, Suffolk, UK.

The Sleep of Reason Creates Monsters The poem takes its title from an etching by Francisco Goya. It was also suggested by a card-playing trope from the poem *Cabhair Ní Ghairfead* by Aogán Ó Rathaille.

During Donald Trump's Inauguration On May 18, 1952, Paul Robeson performed an outdoor concert for more than 25,000 people gathered on both sides of the United States/Canadian border at Peace Arch Park in Blaine, Washington State. His passport had been confiscated by the State Department.

In a Walled Garden Written after a number of visits to *Le Mémorial des Martyrs de la Déportation*, a memorial to the 200,000 Jews deported from Vichy France to the Nazi concentration camps during World War II. It is located below ground level behind the Cathedral of Notre Dame on Île de la Cité, Paris.

Dance of the City Written in response to *La Danse* by Henri Matisse (Musée d'Art Moderne de la Ville de Paris).

Badhbh Written in response to the painting *La Guerre (War)* by Henri Rousseau (Musée d'Orsay, Paris). The title is a Gaelic word that combines the meanings of 'carrion crow' and 'war goddess'.

Light Two paintings lie behind this poem: *Guernica* by Pablo

Picasso (Museo Reina Sofía, Madrid) and *The Third of May 1808* by Francisco Goya (Museo del Prado, Madrid).

Piobrachd Written in response to the playing of *Gol na mBan san Ár* by the piper David Power, as played on his CD *The Eighteen Moloney.*

The White Bear Written in response to a sculpture of the same name by François Pompon (Musée d'Orsay, Paris).

War Pipes Suggested by the legend behind the Scottish Gaelic song *Uamh an Òir,* as sung and played on the CD *Fhuair Mi Pòg* by Margaret Stewart & Allan MacDonald, as well as by the poem of the same name by Somhairle Mac Gill-Eain (Sorley MacLean).

IV

Family Meal Written in response to the painting *Dinner by Lamplight* by Félix Valloton (Musée d'Orsay, Paris).

A Postcard from Knossos Written after a visit to the site of the palace at Knossos, Crete.

Faustina Shivers Written after a conflict between bureaucracy and the arts, a conflict in which everybody lost, including the bureaucracy personnel. I do not wish to be more specific.

Triptych for a Neighbour Suggested by a plaster-cast buddha that overlooks the sea from a small cliff at the end of my garden.

The Bell for Order Suggested by the song *The Castle of Dromore,* as sung by the late Eamon Langford of Kells, Co. Kerry.

Candle Suggested by a paschal candle seen in St. Mark's English Church, Florence.

The Configuration of Love Suggested by sections of the orchestral suite *The Planets,* by Gustav Holst.

A Bracelet from Florence Written to accompany a silver bracelet I bought on the Ponte Vecchio, Florence.

Afternoon Pilgrimage *Santo André de Teixido* is a pilgrimage village among the cliffs of the coast of Galicia, northwest Spain.

In a Hammock in Galicia Suggested by *An Lebor Gabála,* the mythological conquest of Ireland by Amergin and the Milesians from Galicia.

The Place of Prayer Written in response to *Six Prayers*, a tapestry woven as a Holocaust memorial by Anni Albers, and which was part of a 2018 exhibition of her work at the Tate Modern Gallery (London).

Amergin's Ship Written to mark the erection of the bronze sculpture *Árthach Dána*, by Holger Lönze, in Waterville, Co. Kerry to mark the landing place of Amergin and the Milesian or Gaelic people, as related in the mythological *Lebor Gabála.*

Shaping the Place of Speech Written after a talk entitled *Amairgen and Ireland's Myth of Itself,* by John Carey, at the 2019 Amergin Solstice Poetry Gathering in Waterville, Co. Kerry.

Dance Written in response to *Carbon, time and space*, a multimedia installation created in 2017/18 by Karen Hendy while she was artist-in-residence in Siamsa Tíre, Tralee, Co. Kerry.

The Dispute about the Immaculate Conception Written in response to a painting of the same name by Carlo Portelli in the Basilica di Santa Croce, Florence.

Pietà Written in response to a painting by Mícheál Ua Ciarmhaic, a reproduction of which can be seen in the anthology *Duanaire Mhaidhcí,* ed. Paddy Bushe (Coiscéim, 2006).

The Road to God Knows Where Written in response to a painting of the same name by Seán Hardie.

Listener Written in response to *Écoute,* a sculpture by Henri de Miller beside the Church of St-Eustache in Paris.

Solstice Written after a Midwinter Day reading at the Íochtar Cua Alignment, a Bronze Age megalithic alignment near Waterville, Co. Kerry.

Midwinter Sunset, Cill Rialaig A low stone passageway leading to the principal cell in the remains of the Early Medieval monastery at Cill Rialaig on Bolus Head in Co. Kerry was aligned on the setting sun at the midwinter solstice.

Casting Written after a 2018 gathering in Cillín Liath, Co. Kerry, of *Umha Aois*, a group of artists, archaeologists and others interested in exploring the working methods of Bronze Age craftworkers.

Sky Woman Written after several visits to *Femmes en Mouvement*, a 2015 exhibition of paintings by the Japanese artist Aya Takagi at the Université Paris Descartes exhibition centre.

Woman, Moon and Mountain Written in response to a tapestry woven by the artist Lisbeth Mulcahy.

The Piper Abroad Written in response to the piping of Ailean Dòmhnullach (Allan MacDonald), especially but not exclusively in response to *Chrò Chinn t-Sàile,* often known by its first line *Thèid mi dhachaidh/ I will go home,* a song found on the CD *Fhuair Mi Pòg* by Margaret Stewart & Allan MacDonald.

Forging Icarus Written in response to *Large Icarus*, a sculpture by Fritz Koenig which was included in a 2018 exhibition of his work at the Palazzo Pitti, Florence.

First Day in Varnam Written sitting beside the lotus pond at Varnam Homestay, Kerala, India in February 2018.

Turning the Tune Written in response to the guitarist Steve Cooney's playing of *Tabhair Dom do Lámh*, a 17th century composition by the harpist Ruaidhrí Dall Ó Catháin.

DEDALUS PRESS

SECOND SIGHT

PADDY BUSHE

ZDTNUHP

HPXTZFN

DEDALUS

Poems in Irish, with English translations by the author

dom bhean feasa

ACKNOWLEDGEMENTS

The poems gathered here appeared in the collections *In Ainneoin na gCloch, Gile na Gile* and *Móinéar an Chroí,* all published by Coiscéim. The author is grateful for the commitment and energy which Pádraig Ó Snodaigh has devoted to that press for many years, and particularly for the personal encouragement received. *Gura fada buan an fear agus an cló.*

SECOND SIGHT

poems in Irish
with English translations by the author

PADDY BUSHE

DEDALUS PRESS

I

Cárta Poist ón Himalaya

Beir beannacht uaim, a scríbhinn,
Ó bheannta arda Tarapani
Go Mín a' Léith faoin Earagail
Is go Cathal caoin Ó Searcaigh.

Bí-se ar foluain mar bhrat urnaí
Os cionn an bhrait ghil sneachta,
Agus seol mo scéal na mílte siar
Om mani padme ohm do mhantra.

Aimsigh bratacha urnaí an fhile
Á searradh féin chun scéal a chlos;
Cogair-se draíocht na mbeann ard leo,
Agus buíochas croí ón bhfile Bushe.

Feabhra, 2007

A Postcard from the Himalaya

Carry herewith my heartfelt blessing
From the snowy heights of Tarapani,
To Mín a' Léith below Errigal
And to Cathal *caoin* Ó Searcaigh.

Hover like an airy prayer-flag
Above this downy blanket,
Then send my story far far west,
Om mani padme ohm your mantra.

Search out the poet's own prayer-flags,
All agog for the east wind's offering,
Whisper to them of high peak magic
And the poet Bushe's *gúrú maith agat.*

February 2007

Síscéal

Chuir an Chailleach Ghlic an gheal
Ina dubh ar Kathmandu, d'iompaigh
An dealán ina chith mharfach, chas
Deiseal ina thuathal, thiontaigh
An grá ina ghruaim, agus leath
Brat bréagach ar lomchlár na fírinne.

Ach *bistari, bistari*. Fillfidh an feall
Ar an gCailleach Ghlic, scaipfear
Doircheacht an cheo nimhe a d'ardaigh sí,
Scaoilfear an ceangal a shnaidhm sí
Ar chúig caol na fírinne, agus beidh
An dubh ina gheal ar Kathmandu arís.

Bistari, bistari: "tóg breá bog é" sa Neipeailis.

110

Fairytale

The Sly Old Witch beguiled the light
Of Kathmandu towards dark, concocted
Poisonous rain from sunshine, wrenched
The sun itself from its course, twisted
Love into its own antithesis, and spread
A black cloak of deception over the streets.

But *bistari, bistari.* Betrayal will ineluctably
Come slinking back around the Sly Witch,
The foul mist she conjured will be dissipated,
That web of malevolence wherein she bound
The truth will loosen, and dark will turn
Towards the light once more in Kathmandu.

"Bistari, bistari" is Nepalese for "take your time".

Nóta Cágach do Chathal

I gcathair Kathmandu arís, agus na préacháin úd
I gciorcail os mo chionn, meabhraíodh dom in athuair

Gurb ionann "cág" na Gaeilge agus "kaag" na háite seo
Agus rith sé liom gur cinnte go n-aithneodh cág

Cág díoltasach eile cuma fada gearr óna chéile iad
Agus gur ró-dhócha go mbainfidís araon sásamh

Agus sú mar a chéile as súile claona na Caillí Bréagaí
A stracadh glan as a ceann, in aon teanga ar domhan.

Kathmandu, 15 Feabhra 2018

A Raucous Note to Cathal

In Kathmandu again, with those familiar crows
Circling overhead, I'm reminded once more

That the Gaelic *cág* is the same bird as *kaag* here
And I guess that any crow would surely recognise

Another vengeful crow at no matter what distance
And they would find common and deep satisfaction

In plucking the malign eyes of any wicked witch
Clean out of her head, in any language on earth.

Kathmandu, 15 February 2018

Bé Ghlas d'Orsay

*do Chathal Ó Searcaigh, i ndiaidh clár-dhealbh
le Georges Lacombe*

Seo chugat í, a fhile, seo chugat
  Bé ghlas úd na coille, í ar maos
    Le h-úire, le glaise na coille.

Seo chugat í, ina steillebheatha adhmaid
  Ag stealladh beatha chomh beo chéanna
    Leis an ndán a d'fhógair tú in ómós di.

Seo chugat í, *ballán cíche i mbarr féithe* do dháin
  Greanta go snoite anseo, ag tál flúirseacht fola
    Ar chré is ar phréamh, ar ghas is ar chrann.

Seo chugat í, na cuacha donnrua uirthi
  Ag caisiú anuas trí ithir, agus siar
    Suas arís trí luibh is dris is coirt.

Seo chugat í, ar tinneall le deirge na gcaor
  Ar crith le h-éadroime na nduilleog
    Ar meisce le meidhreacht na n-éan.

Seo chugat í, ar strae le buile an ghiorria
  Ar foluain le rince roithleánach na gaoithe
    Ar cosa in airde rábach a graostachta.

Seo chugat í, a stathfadh an dá shúil
  As aon chailleach bhréagach a leagfadh
    Leathshúil chlaon ort chun do chluainte.

114

The Green Goddess of Orsay

after a relief sculpture in wood by Georges Lacombe
for Cathal Ó Searcaigh

See, poet, she comes towards you,
  Your own woodland deity, moist
    With the wood's mossy greenness.

See, she is ingrained in her own living image,
  Brimming over with the same *joie de vivre*
    As the poem that proclaimed your devotion.

See, with her *nipple swelling from the vein,*
  She is carved proud here, pouring abundance
    Onto clay and roots, into stems and trunks.

See, the waves of her chestnut hair
  Flow down through clay, then curl
    Upward again in leaf and briar and bark.

See, she is intense with the redness of berries
  Quivering with the weightlessness of leaves
    High as a kite with the wingding of birds.

See, she is astray with the madness of hares
  Afloat on the dizzy height of the wind's dance
    Away on the wild gallop of her own bawdiness.

See, she comes, who would tear the eyes
  Out of any deceiving witch who would cast
    A foul eye on you to beguile you into harm's way.

Seo chugat í, faoi éide chatha,
　Ór an aitinn, corcra an fhraoigh
　　Faoi réir chun cogadh na talún.

Seo chugat í, cnó agus caor i dtaisce
　Mar lón cogaidh in n-aghaidh siúd
　　Nach ndéanann urnaí sa choill.

Seo chugat í, ar mhór léi riamh
　Do bhunadh féin, cé gur shealbhaíodar
　　No man's land na gcuibhreann uaithi.

Seo chugat í, cumhracht ar sileadh léi
　I bhfleascanna féithlinn, a cuacha
　　Lúbtha le creamh is le raideog.

Seo chugat í, a fhile. Sí do bheatha.
　Go mbeannaítear laethanta bhur gcaidrimh.
　　I bhfochair a chéile, go ngine sibh marthanacht.

Oíche na SeanBhliana, 2016

116

See, she comes to you dressed for battle
   In the gold of furze, in the purple of heather
      Arrayed for combat in the war for the land.

See, she comes with nuts and berries
   Rations squirreled away for war against those
      Who do not observe the sanctity of woods.

See, she comes who always esteemed
   Your own people, although they appropriated
      The no man's land of the small fields from her.

See, she comes trailing fragrance
   In garlands of woodbine, her hair
      Twined with wild garlic, bog-myrtle.

See, poet. She comes to you who gave you life.
   May the days of your disclosures bring blessings.
      May your communion beget that which will continue.

New Year's Eve, 2016

Aonghas Úrghlas ag 70

do Aonghas Dubh MacNeacail

So what má tá an dubh curtha go snasta ina gheal ort
Ag an aimsir? Ní raibh dul amú ort riamh faoi ghile

Nó doircheacht na cruinne, agus níor nós leat taobhú
Le dearcadh dubh-is-bán na súl géar úd atá dall

Ar an gcrotal glasuaithne i léithe na carraige,
Dall ar ildaiteacht gach ní inár dtimpeall,

Agus bodhar ar iliomad leagan an scéil
Atá á chanadh gan tús gan deireadh ar fud na cruinne.

A Aonghais Dhuibh, a Aonghais Ghil, a ghlaise úir:
Lean ort ag boilgearnach thar maoil na dteorainneacha uile.

Nár ruga riamh ceartchreideamhacht ort, is nár thaga ort
Mór-is-fiú na gceannlitreacha nó saoithíneacht na lánstad.

Evergreen Aonghas at 70

for Aonghas Dubh MacNeacail

So what if time has belied you, and turned those jet
Locks white? You were never one to deny the light

Or the dark of the world. But neither did you give in
To the black and white vision, to those who are blind

To the viridescent lichen in the greyness of the rock,
Blind to the colour that saturates our surroundings,

And deaf to all the tellings of the story constantly
Sung without beginning or end all over the world.

Aonghas Dubh. Aonghas Geal. Green-reflecting wellspring:
Never stop bubbling over the brim of all the boundaries,

Never let the orthodox catch up on you, nor let yourself suffer
The self-importance of the capital, the pedantry of the full stop.

Ómós do Shomhairle MacGill-Eain

Thig crìoch air an t-saoghal ach mairidh ceòl is gaol

Bóithrín a bhí réaltach le nóiníní
A thionlaic sinn go dtí Hallaig,
Á shní féin go héasca
Suas idir faill agus farraige.

Leanamar ar an gcaonach caoin
Loirg crúibe agus coise,
Céim ar chéim sciorrach
Le fia agus le file.

D'aithris an ghaoth sáile
Aníos ó bharr na dtonnta
Bhéarsaí i measc craobhacha
Lán srónaíl agus sondais.

Chuir beann is ailt is creag
Cluas orthu féin le héisteacht
Agus chiúnaigh cliotar na dtaibhsí
I measc coll is beith is caorthainn.

Bhraith neantóg is driseog bíog
I gclocha na bhfothrach fúthu
Is glór an bhaird ag séideadh
Síol na tine sa luaithreach.

Agus bhain urchar grá macalla
As an aer mórthimpeall Hallaig
Is bhí an aimsir chaite láithreach
Beo le mná is le fearaibh.

120

Homage to Sorley MacLean

There comes an end to the world, but none to music, nor to love

It was a pathway stellar with daisies
That conveyed us into Hallaig
Winding its fluent way
Up between sea and crag.

On the kindly moss we followed
The prints of foot and hoof,
Step by slippery step
With a deer, with a poet.

The salty wind recited
From the wavetops below
Verses between the branches,
Nasal and sonorous.

Summit and cliff and crag
Settled themselves to listen,
And the chatter of ghosts softened
Among hazels, rowans, birches.

Nettles and briars felt a stirring
In the ruins their roots encircled,
As bardic utterance awakened
The spark in dormant embers.

And a bullet of love resounded
In the air surrounding Hallaig
While the past tense became present
With the bustle of men and women.

Sciúrd faoi Screapadal

do Meg Bateman

Bhí fiolar ar thóir creiche dar dtionlacan,
Ar foluain os cionn na bhfothrach ciúin,

An lá niamhrach earraigh sin gur shiúlamar
Fad le Screapadal, ar lorg dhán Shomhairle

Agus scáileanna Tharmaid is Eachainn Mhòir
Ag breathnú anonn ar Chomraich Ma Ruibhe.

Ach níor ardaigh aon tuiréad sleamhain dubh
É féin go bagarthach trí chrothloinnir na farraige,

Is níor bhodhraigh sianáil aon scaird-bhuamaire
Méiligh na n-uan agus portaireacht na n-éan

Fad a dheineamar dán Shomhairle a reic,
Gàidhlig agus Gaeilge, os ard i measc tithe bánaithe.

I bhfianaise an tseanchaisleáin a thit le faill,
Agus Carraig na hEaglaise Bréige scoite ón dtalamh;

In ainneoin na gceannlínte ós na ceithre h-arda,
Sotal rachmasóirí agus slad an mhargaidh;

I bhfianaise na gcaorach caidéiseach ar fhallaí
Agus féile na gréine ar fhiailí is ar fhásach;

In ainneoin bhréaginsint na scéalaithe
A scaipeann scéalta de réir toil na máistrí;

Ba bheag ná go gcreidfeá go raibh deireadh i ndán
Don tsaint, don chos-ar-bholg agus don gcreach.

A Quick Trip into Screapadal

for Meg Bateman

An eagle scanning for spoil accompanied us,
Circling high above the silent ruined houses,

That magical spring day when we walked
To Screapadal, tracking Somhairle's poem

While the shades of Tarmad and Eachann Mòr
Stared across the sound to Comraich Ma Ruibhe.

But today no sleek black turret raised its ominous
Presence above the sea's shimmering surface,

And no howling of a jet-bomber drowned out
The bleating of lambs or the piping of birds

As we declaimed Somhairle's poem aloud,
Gàidhlig and Gaeilge, among the shells of houses.

In light of the castle disintegrating down the cliff
And of False Church Rock lying just offshore;

In spite of headlines from the earth's four corners,
The swagger of wealth and the pillage of the markets;

In the light of inquisitive sheep climbing on walls
And benevolent sunshine on weeds and wasteland;

In spite of false tales spread by narrators
Who tailor the news to the will of their masters;

You could almost imagine rhyming a farewell
To greed, to exploitation, to the frenzy for spoil.

Lagtrá

Tá an trá folamh.
Macallaí beaga ag plopadh
Idir fheamainn is carraig.

Anois tá báirnigh ag tnúth
Le mná malla dubha
Aoine an Chéasta.

Níl aon tsolas ón Sceilg.
Tá sé ráite i gcónaí
Go mbeidh coinneal dubh
Ós comhair gach tí.

Tá an tarbh i dTeach Duinn
Ag fógairt ceo; ag fógairt
Trí lagsholas an tráthnóna
Go gcleachtófar arís
Fíogaigh is ruacain abhann.

Stranded

An empty shoreline.
Small plopping echoes
Between seaweed and rock.

Now limpets hold their breath
For the dark, stately
Women of Good Friday.

There is no beam from Skellig.
It is still said
There will be a black candle
Beside every house.

The bull in Teach Duinn
Is trumpeting fog; trumpeting
Through the thin evening light
That we will subsist again
On dogfish, scrapings from shells.

An Mhuintir agus an Éigse

do Ba Da Chai

De thaisme, más ann in aon chor dá leithéid,
A bhuaileamar, mise ar shiúlóid maidne,
Tusa ag dúnadh dorais. *This my study house.*
What do you study? Make poems. So do I.
Agus away linn díreach go dtí an scoil filíochta agat
(*Peoples and Poems* a d'aistrís an t-ainm le scairt)
Ar bhruach an chuain. Seomra geal, fairsing,
Boird agus mataí ina n-áiteanna féin,
Agus druma mór chun rithime ar an urlár

B'fhada fada sinn ó sheomraí dorcha
Agus clocha ar bhrollach gach ábhar file.
Gach aon fhuinneog níos niamhraí ná a chéile:
Sliogiascairí i gcrithloinnir an lagtrá,
Nóra na bPortach agus éirí-níos-airde uirthi
Leis an gclúmh geal bán a fuair sí anseo timpeall,
Agus Ilch'ubong, Mullach Éirí na Gréine,
Ag taibhreamh ar thine a spalpadh amach arís
Ach an lá a bheith róbhrothallach.

Mhalairtíomar leabhair go deasghnáthúil
Agus d'ólamar té glas go deasghnáthúil,
(Agus ba dheas, gnáthúil mar a dheineamar)
Inár suí go ciarógach ag bord íseal,
Ag tabhairt aitheantais chuí dá chéile.
Agus cé gur bhrathas ar dtús iartharach, tuathalach,
Fiú corrthónach, d'éiríos diaidh ar ndiaidh
Suaimhneach, oirthearach, fiú Searcenstockach,
In Songsan, i dtigh geal sin na filíochta.

Peoples and Poems

for Ba Da Chai

It was by chance, if there is any such thing,
That we met, me out for a morning walk,
You closing a front door. *This my study house.*
What do you study? Make poems. So do I!
And away with us to your school of poetry
(*Peoples and Poems*, you translated the name, laughing)
On the edge of the sea. A lucent, airy room,
Tables and floor-mats, each in its own space,
And a skin drum invoking rhythm on the floor.

We were miles and miles from darkened rooms
And bardic apprentices with stones on their chests.
Each window framed more magic than the next:
Shellfish-gatherers in the shimmering ebb-tide,
Nora the Bog getting even more stuck-up
With the dazzling white outfit she picked up around here,
And *Ilch'ubong*, the Summit of the Rising Sun,
Dreaming about erupting one more time,
Only that the day was far too warm.

We ceremoniously exchanged our books
And drank green tea, again ceremoniously,
(And the ceremony was marvellously everyday)
As we sat cross-legged at a low table,
Eyeing each other with due recognition,
And although I was awkward and western,
You could even say tight-arsed, I became inch by inch
Easier, more oriental, (dare I say Searcenstockian?)
In *Songsan*, in that luminous house of poetry.

Carraig Taibhrimh

Déantar carraig díom,
Carraig taibhrimh.

Tagadh saoithe faram
Ag saothrú eolais.

Tagadh an óige faram
Ag cuartú rúndachta.

Bíom bodhar, ag éisteacht
Le cliotar na réalta.

Bíom balbh, ag suirí
Le deisbhéalaíocht na gaoithe.

Déantar carraig díom,
Carraig snoite le haois.

Stone Dreaming

Let me be stone
Stone dreaming.

Let sages approach me
Scraping for knowledge.

Let youth approach me
In search of secrecy.

Let me be deaf, listening
To the chattering of stars.

Let me be mute, flirting
With the sweet talk of the wind.

Let me be stone
Stone chiselled with age.

An Eachtra Nua

i.m. Dónal Mac Síthigh

Abair, a mhairnéalaigh, ó sciobadh mar sin do bhád
Gan choinne amach thar imeall farraige agus tíre
I dtreo críocha bruadaracha úd na scéal is na laoch;

Abair, a ródaí, cá fada an turas ón dtonn mhallaithe,
Fad na dubhchríche ceobhránaí seo nach bhfuil ann
Le fírinne, nó as; cá fada go gcruthófar do chló ceart,

Ar ráiniú duit gealchríoch na heachtraíochta, go ndéanfar
Áit duit cois teallaigh led léathbhádóirí, go gcloisfear thú
Cruinn glan, gan chaoineadh eadránach seo na droinge?

Géaraigh do choiscéim, a fhánaí. Táthar santach chun scéil.
Ón ard nua mar a bheir, abair amach an eachtra a mhairfidh
Ó Shamhain amach go Bealtaine is ó Bhealtaine ar ais arís.

14 Samhain 2017

A New Epic

i.m. Danny Sheehy

Say, mariner, since that your boat was so capriciously
Swept beyond the utmost borders of sea and sky
To that dreamlike territory of stories and heroes;

Say, voyager, how far it is from that malevolent wave
Through this obscure, vaporous land that is, in truth,
Neither here nor there; how long before your true form

Makes landfall on that legendary shore, before you take
Your place at the fireside of your peers and are heard
Clear and true above this transitory mourning of the tribe?

Sharpen your pace, traveller. There is a thirst for storytelling.
From your new elevation, recount an epic that will last
From *Samhain* to *Bealtaine*, and from *Bealtaine* back again.

14 November 2017

Cloisfead Ar Neamh

Über Sternen muß er wohnen – Schiller

Bhí Beethoven ar an steiréo, an tigh
Tonnchreathach, líonreathach, gairdeach,

Agus mé ar tí dul ag bothántaíocht
Go dtí mo chomharsa. Níor mhúchas an ceol

Agus d'fhágas dóirse agus fuinneoga ar leathadh
Nuair a shiúlas amach faoi ghile oíche sheaca.

Gotha an stiúrthóra orm, bheannaíos
Go mórchúiseach le ceolfhoireann na réalt,

Sheolas an uile nóta chucu, agus shiúlas liom
Ag súil gur chualathas an ceol ar neamh.

I Shall Hear in Heaven

Über Sternen muß er wohnen – Schiller

I had Beethoven on the stereo, the house
Wave-shaking, full-flowing, celebrating,

When I took a notion to go rambling
To my neighbour. I left the music playing

And the doors and windows wide open
As I walked out into the frosty starlight.

Throwing shapes like a conductor, I bowed
Ceremoniously to the orchestra of the stars,

Signalled every last note to them, and walked on,
Hoping the music would be heard in Heaven.

II

An Manach, na Lachain agus an Loch

Ní fhacas féin ach sraith ghriangrafanna,
Ach ó lámhchomharthaí an ghrianghrafadóra
Maraon le cúpla focal a chompánaigh,
Thuigeas gurbh i bhfad i bhfad siar ó thuaidh
Ar Ardán na Tibeite lena 4x4 a bhíodar
Nuair a thángadar ar an manach is a scuaine,
É siúd go cúramach ag treorú lachan agus a h-ál
I dtreo locha bhí ina luí faoi bheanna sneachta.
Gur thuigeadar uaidh go raibh sé féin
I mbun oileathrachta fada sna críocha sin
Nuair a tháinig sé orthu, i bhfad ón uisce.
Go raibh sé tar éis a dhéanamh amach
Gur neadaigh an lacha tamaillín roimhe sin
Ar imeall an locha, ach de bharr athrú obann
Sa tséasúr, tuile nó tirimeacht éigin
A d'imigh thar tuiscint manach nó lacha,
Gur chúlaigh an loch i bhfad siar ón nead,
Agus nuair a rugadh an t-ál ar deireadh,
Nach raibh faic in aon chor ina dtimpeall
Ach cré leath-reoite, clochach. Dá bhrí sin,
Go raibh sé féin ag briseadh a oilithreachta
(D'fhéadfadh sé siúl níos tapúla ina dhiaidh sin)
Is á mbeathú is a mealladh is á bpeataireacht
I dtreo an locha, mar nár mhaith leis
Roth a mbeatha a fheiscint ag imeacht i léig.

Rianaigh na grianghrafanna an scéal
Céim ar chéim go dtí gur shroicheadar
Ceann scríbe, agus gur sheas an manach
Faoi ghoirme spéir reoite an Earraigh
Ar bhruach locha a bhí chomh fairsing sin
Go sílfeá gur sheas sé ar bhruach an domhain.

The Monk, the Ducks and the Lake

To be honest I myself saw only some photographs,
But from the sign-language of the photographer
Together with his friend's few words of English,
I made out it was in the far northwestern part
Of the Tibetan plateau they had been in their 4x4
When they came across this monk and his flock,
The monk carefully escorting a duck and her brood
Towards a lake under distant, snowy summits;
That they understood from him that he had been
Undertaking a long pilgrimage through these parts
When he came across the ducks, far from water;
That he had concluded, after much thought,
That a duck and drake had nested some time before
At the lake's edge, but because of some change
Or other in the season, some drought or flood
Beyond the understanding of either monks or ducks,
That the lake had retreated far from the nest,
And when the now drakeless duck hatched the eggs
There was nothing at all visible around them
But stony, half-frozen clay. And so, he told them,
He was interrupting his pilgrimage for the time being
(He could always walk a little faster afterwards)
And feeding them and quacking them and coaxing them
Towards the lake, because he couldn't bear to see
The wheel of their small duck-lives run down.

The photographs tracked the rest of the story
Step by guided, waddling step until they reached
Their destination, and the robed monk stood
Under the freezing blue sky of Spring
At the shore of a lake that stretched so far
You'd think he stood at the wide world's edge.

Agus cé na faca féin faic eile,
Tá tuairim agam gur leá criostal
I ndiaidh chriostail ghil oighir
Ar an sliabh, agus gur chromadar
Ag plimpeáil leo ceann ar cheann
Anuas sa mhullach ar a chéile
Ag sruthú leo i dtreo an locha,
Go raibh aoibh na n-aoibh ar an manach
Is é ag dordadh sútra ar an mbruach,
Ag guí leis na lachain ag lapadaíl sa láib,
Leis an roth ag rothaíocht ina cheart arís.

And although I saw or heard nothing else,
I have this strange notion that crystal
After crystal of gleaming ice melted
High up on the mountain, and began
Plinking and plinking, each one dropping
Slowly down onto another after another,
Gathering themselves to flow to the lake;
That the monk's smile was wide as the world
As he stood and droned a sutra on the shore,
Praying with the ducks' delighted dabbling,
With the wheel spinning at its own speed again.

Fuaimrian

Tá sé ag rith is ag ath-rith
Trím aigne: blúire de scannán
Dubh agus bán creathánach
Ar chlár thromchúiseach teilifíse.

Na caogaidí. An tSín. Mao.
An Léim Mhór Chun Tosaigh.
Cruach á bruithniú go craosach
As seanúirlisí i sráidbhailte
Ó cheann ceann na tíre,
Agus an ghráin dhearg ag an bPáirtí
Ar éanacha beaga ceoil
As gach aon ghráinne cruithneachtan
A ghoideann siad idir portanna.

Sluaite á mbailiú, mar sin,
Ag gach aon chúinne sráide
Agus bualadh ollmhór oifigiúil bos,
Á spreagadh gan stad le gártha cáinte,
Ag cur na ceoltóirí beaga de gheit
Ag eitilt timpeall agus timpeall arís
Go dtí go dtiteann, ar deireadh, éan
Ar éan de phlimp i ndiaidh a chéile,
Traochta chun báis ar an dtalamh.

Níl aon fhuaimrian ceoil
Leis an scannán. Ach samhlaím
Na mílte fliútanna aeracha bambú
Ag boilgearnach leo scathaimhín,
Agus, poll ar pholl, nóta ar nóta,
Samhlaím gob ollmhór dubh á sárú
Chun chiúnais, ceann ar cheann.

Soundtrack

It's running and rerunning
In my mind: a short loop,
Shaky, black and white,
From some weighty documentary.

The fifties. China. Mao.
The Great Leap Forward.
Steel hungrily smelted
From scrap in villages
The length and breadth of the country,
And the Party's official hatred
Of all small songbirds
For every last grain of wheat
They steal between songbursts.

Crowds therefore marshalled
At every street corner
And a huge sanctioned burst of handclapping
To raise morale with catcalls of denunciation,
Startling the little songsters into flight
Around and around and around again
Until, in the end, one by one and thud
By thud they fall after each other,
Exhausted to bits on the ground.

There's no soundtrack
To the film. But I conjure up
Thousands of giddy bamboo flutes
Bubbling away for a while,
Until, stop by stop, note by note,
One huge black beak cows them
Into silence, one by one.

Agus samhlaím ina n-áit
Trúmpa mór amháin práis
Ag búireadh an nóta chéanna
Lá i ndiadh lae i ndiaidh lae.

And I imagine in their place
One enormous brass trumpet
Bellowing the same note
Day after day after day.

Ag an Droichead a Cruthaíodh ar Neamh

Tá mar a bheadh loirg cos brúite anseo san aolchloch,
Paidreacha greanta ar leaca, agus cuimhne ag an gcarraig
Ar scéal scéil faoi thuras go dtí an Domhan Thiar
D'fhonn eagna Bhúda a bhreith abhaile ón Ind.

Thar teorainn anseo a thángadar, na h-oilithrigh,
Ag cuartú na dtrí ciseán, Dlí, Agallamh agus Scrioptúr,
Is athnuachan ar smior na gcnámh, ar fhuil na feola.
Manach i mbláth a aithbhreithe, agus rógaire saoi de mhoncaí

A chothaigh, de bharr daonnacht a dhéithiúileachta,
Agus ainmhíocht neamhthruaillithe a dhaonnachta,
Raic i bPálás Neimhe, iontas ar Shealúchas an Chré,
Agus borradh nua in Impireacht na Marbh.

Ag an droichead Neamhdhéanta seo idir dhá ríocht,
D'fhág gach aon deamhan is drochrud is dragún
A bhí á gciapadh go dtí sin, faoiseamh acu ar deireadh,
Agus ghluaiseadar le leoithne cumhra trí úllghoirt fairsinge.

Teanntaithe idir failltreacha, tá an abhainn
Ina tuile buí ag réabadh thar charraigreacha,
Agus uisce ón lochán gaile lena h-ais
Ag beiriú ón dtalamh trínachéile laistíos.

Tá an áirse ollmhór cloiche os ár gcionn
Ag fáisceadh na bhfailltreacha lena chéile,
Is ag rá: *Ní bheifear scartha. In ainneoin teorainneacha,
A thaistealaithe, tá sibh i gcríocha na droicheadúileachta*

At the Bridge Made in Heaven

Here are footprints of legend in the limestone,
Prayers carved on slabs, the rock still remembering
A tale told of a journey to the Western World
To bring back from India the wisdom of the Buddha.

Here they crossed borders, those pilgrims who sought
The three baskets of Law, Dialogue and Scripture
And renewal of the bone's marrow, the flesh's blood:
A venerable monk, a sly pig and a wise rogue of a monkey

Whose constant shifting between humanity of his divinity
And the unadulterated simianism of his humanity,
Caused uproar in Heaven, amazement on Earth,
And fresh stirrings in the Kingdom of the Dead.

Here at this Heaven-made bridge between kingdoms,
Those devils, dragons and other damnable beings
Who had tormented them, left them at last
To travel in peace through fragrant orchards.

Confined between canyon walls, the river
Is a yellow flood thundering over boulders,
While the water in the thermal pool close by
Steams and bubbles with subterranean agitation.

The huge arch of rock stretching overhead
Spans the canyon, squeezing its walls together,
Saying: *There will be no severance. In spite of borders,
Travellers, you have arrived in the realm of bridges.*

Ag Aistriú 'Buddha in der Glorie'

In aghaidh mo thola, bhí sé caite uaim agam,
An smaoineamh go n-aistreoinn an dán sin le Rilke,
Cé go raibh sé fillte agus aithfhillte tr ím aigne
Mar a bheadh bratóg urnaithe ar chrann naofa.

Fuaireas róchoimhthíoch iad, na críocha úd
Ina raibh an dán agus an t-aistriúchán ag taisteal,
An ghramadach débhríoch, agus nósmhaireacht an táirsigh
Suite mar chonstaic ar mo chead isteach.

Ach nuair a bhaineas mo bhróga iartharacha díom
Roimh gabháil thar táirseach Teampall Prah Singh,
Is nuair a shuíos croschosach ag análú tiúise,
Cloigíní ag bualadh i leoithne anseo is ansiúd,

D'aithníos Búda Rilke os mo chomhair in airde,
Ceannbhrat naoi gciseal go caithréimeach
Ar foluain os a chionn. I loinnir an íomhá,
Thuigeas go bhféadfaí go ndéanfaí teanga díom.

Translating 'Buddha in Der Glorie'

Against my will, I had put to one side
The notion of translating that poem by Rilke,
Despite it winding itself around my mind
Like prayer-flags around a sacred tree.

They were too alien to me, those territories
Where poem and translation were travelling;
The grammar ambiguous, and the threshold customs
Squatting like portal guards against my entering.

But when I took off my occidental shoes
Before crossing the threshold of Wat Phrah Singh,
And when I sat, cross-legged, inhaling incense,
Temple bells tinkling somewhere in the breeze,

I recognised Rilke's *Buddha* high up before me,
A nine-tiered canopy triumphantly floating
Above his head. In that resplendent image
Gleamed the possibility of the gift of tongues.

Corra Bána

do Éanna

Bhí sé beagnach dearmadta agam, an crann sin
A chonac ón mbus, taobh amuigh de bhaile,
É breac le corra bána suite mar a bheadh éarlais
Ar ghrástúlacht, fad saoil agus bheith ann don eile.

Fad saoil chugat féin, mar sin, a rug abhaile
Ód chuid taistil féin an bhratóg shíoda,
Deartha leis na héin rathúla chéanna
A thuirling im aigne le cleitearnach aoibhinn.

Agus tá siad neadaithe i gcónaí faram,
Ag saibhriú an tseomra le cumhracht na Síne,
Suite gan bhogadh ar ghiúis is ar charraig.
Is nuair a chraitheann an bhratóg i bpuithín gaoithe,

Cloisim, ar feadh soicind, mionabhar na síoraíochta
Sa leoithne éadrom ag siosarnach trín síoda.

White Egrets

for Éanna

It had almost slipped my mind, that tree
I glimpsed once from a trundling bus,
Dappled with egrets like long-standing promises
Of grace, long life and the truth of otherness.

So long life to you too, for bringing home
From your own travels, this painted silk
Bright with those same auspicious birds,
To land in my mind on exhilarated wings.

And they nest still on the sitting-room wall,
Endowing the room with wealth from the east,
Perched now for good on rocks among pine-trees,
And when the scroll stirs in a sudden breeze,

I hear for a moment in that passing wind
Murmurs of eternity rustling through the silk.

Scéal na gCapall

Capaill ag taibhsiú aníos as an gceo
Is ag síothlú arís in airde,
Crú ag clingeadh anseo is ansiúd
Ar charraig, sciorradh tobann
Ag sruthán, seitreach míshuaimhneach
Agus sinne míshuaimhneach, aduain,
Ag luascadh sa diallait, an sliabh
Ag luascadh romhainn agus fúinn
Sa cheo, agus suas linn agus suas
Siar isteach in eachtraíocht.
Cén chreach é seo, cén slad
Lochlannach anuas ar ghleannta,
Cén sága fuilteach atá á chumadh,
Cén Eiric Rua a bhfuil a cháil á reic,
Cén finscéal, fabhalscéal, scéal
Ó Shamhain go Bealtaine Artach é seo?

Go hobann ansin, de gheit
Sriain agus crúibe agus intinne,
Mullach an tsléibhe, an ceo fúinn,
Is mórthimpeall is mórthimpeall,
Gile lom na sléibhte faoin ngréin
Ag síneadh leo go hoighreata
Go ceithre arda an domhain,
Beann ar bheann beag beann
Orainne, ár gcroí inár mbéal,
Ár mbéal faoi thost iontais,
Cluas bodhar orainn do gach
A cumadh nó a ceapadh riamh.

A Tale of Horses

Horses looming out of the mist below
And disappearing upwards again,
A steel shoe ringing here and there
On a rock, abrupt scramblings
At a stream, uneasy snorting
And we also uneasy, strained,
Awkward in our saddles, the mountain
Swaying around and below us
In the fog, then up and again up
And away back into story.
What raid is this, what Viking
Plundering of the valleys,
What bloody epic is being composed,
What Eric the Red's fame narrated,
What story, what saga,
What Arctic winter's tale is this?

All of a sudden, then, with a jerk
Of reins and hooves and minds,
We're up and out, the mist below us,
And around and around and around,
The unfiltered brilliance of the peaks
Stretching themselves icily
To the four corners of the earth,
Summit after summit supremely careless
Of us, of our hearts in our mouths,
Our mouths agape in mute wonder,
And we are stone deaf to any story
Ever recounted since time began.

Giorria Artach

Id staic i logán sléibhe, do dhá chluas
Ar bior, d'fheadfá bheith san airdeall
Ar ghlam gadhar i ngleannta Uíbh Ráthaigh,
Ach go scéitheann dath aolbhán do chóta

Gur sneachta an tuaiscirt is dual agus dúchas duit.
Nó an é an bainne a ghoid an chailleach,
Á dhiúl i riocht ghiorria ó bhuaibh na gcomharsan,
A chlaochlaigh thú go gile sin na gcríoch seo?

Cuma sa tsioc. San iarghúltacht chrua seo
Leánn agus reonn rógaireacht agus leochaileacht
Tríd is tríd a chéile, beag beann ar chora
Tromchúiseacha an tsaoil. Teacht slán is cúram.

Tásc ná tuairisc níl agamsa le coicíos
Ar an saol mór ná ar chinnithe na bhfear
A labhrann le Dia is a labhrann Dia leo
Roimh scaoileadh na mbuamaí, roimh an gol san ár.

Ach ó tá an domhan mar ghiorria idir chonartaibh,
Gach aon bhall ar crith, ag éisteacht faoi sceimhle
Le séideadh adhairce na sealgairí mire
Ar shliabh is ar mhachaire is ar fhásach,

Seo mo ghuí do ghiorria i logán sléibhe sa Ghraonlainn:
Fiolar, faolchú ná ulcabhán nár thaga ort,
Crobh, gob ná fiacal nár ruga riamh ort,
Is ná raibh do chlúmh bán choíche breac led fhuil.

Iúl, 2003

Arctic Hare

Transfixed in a mountain hollow, your ears
All attention, you could be listening out
For baying beagles in Uíbh Ráthach valleys,
Only your lime-white coat cannot conceal

That northern snow is in your blood and breeding.
Or is it the milk that the old witch, taking
The shape of a hare, stole from the neighbours' cows,
Has you morphed into this indigenous brightness?

No matter. In this unyielding remoteness,
Villainy and vulnerability meld one
Into the other, undisturbed by the weighty
Ways of the world. Survival's the thing.

For two weeks now, I've had neither sight nor sound
Of the big world, nor of the decrees of men
Who speak to God and to whom God speaks
Before the bombs' release, the weeping in the slaughter.

But since the world is now a hare between packs,
Trembling in every part, listening in terror
To the bugling of the crazed hunters
Among mountains and plains and deserts,

Here is my wish for this hare in a Greenland hollow:
May no wolf nor owl nor eagle come upon you,
May no tooth nor beak nor talon tear you,
And may your white fur never be dappled with blood.

July, 2003

Búireadh

Beireann oighearshruth lao, adeirtear,
Nuair a scoilteann meall oighir go callánach
Amach uaithi, agus féach ansin romham
Fíord fairsing agus é breac le laonna bána,
A gceann fúthu, ag iníor go suaimhneach
Ar mhachairí míne méithe an tsáile,
Ar ghoirt ghorma ghoirte na farraige.

Ach cad é an búireadh sin a chuala
I gcoim na hoíche aréir, slua-bhúireadh
Mar a bheadh tréad i bpéin? B'shin búir
Oighearchlár mátharach an tréada
Ag lobhadh i dteas buile na cruinne,
Ag cúbadh is ag cúngú is ag leá
I ndeora goirte sáile ár máthar uile.

Bellowing

A glacier calves, the expression has it,
When an iceberg moves noisily
Away out from her, and look: before my eyes
A huge fjord dappled with white calves,
Heads down, grazing peacefully
On smooth, salubrious saline plains,
On the blue, briny grass of the ocean.

But what was that bellowing I heard
In the dead of last night, a mass bellowing
Like a herd in pain? That was the bellowing
Of the herd's maternal icecap
Rotting in the crazed heat of the globe,
Straining and shrinking and melting
In the salt tears of our universal mother.

Aniar Aduaidh

Aniar aduaidh a thiocfaidh sé, an Díle nua,
Beag beann ar Dhia, tubaist dár rogha féin.
Fillfidh ar bhfeall orainn, mall nó luath.

Teas marfach isea feasta an aimsir chrua.
Soineann ina doineann, na séasúir ina gcíreib.
Aniar aduaidh a thiocfaidh sé, an Díle nua.

Goin croí na cruinne, agus fágfar í gan trua.
Meileann oighearshruth go mall, ach meileann go mín réidh.
Fillfidh ár bhfeall orainn, mall nó luath.

Tá geonaíl an oighir ag rá go bhfuiltear chugainn,
Sinn sna críocha déanacha, ag tús agus deireadh ré.
Aniar aduaidh a thiocfaidh sé, an Díle nua.

Baoth anois bheith ag cuardach, baoth bheith ag súil
Le hÁirc ár gConartha le sainnt, conradh nimhnithe an aeir.
Fillfidh ár bhfeall orainn, mall nó luath.

Coimhthíoch a bheifear, ar nós chine aduain
A fhágfar gan tórramh, gan uaigh, gan chré.
Aniar aduaidh a thiocfaidh sé, an Díle nua,
Fillfidh ár bhfeall orainn, mall nó luath.

Out of the Blue

The new Flood will surge, godless, out of the blue
From the northwest, a judgement all our own.
Our treachery will turn on us, late or soon.

Warmth has grown deadly now, sunlight is gloom,
The calm is the storm, the seasons overthrown.
The new Flood will surge, godless, out of the blue.

Wound the world's heart, and she will no longer rue
The glacier grinding slowly, grinding to the bone.
Our treachery will turn on us, late or soon.

The groaning ice announces our impending doom,
The end and start of cycles, a metamorphic zone.
The new Flood will surge, godless, out of the blue.

Too late now for searching, we await like fools
Our Ark of Covenant with greed, our air-poisoning hoard.
Our treachery will turn on us, late or soon.

Our end will be alien, an abandoned crew
Without wake, without grave, without marking stone.
The new Flood will surge, godless, out of the blue.
And our treachery turn on us, late or soon.

Áireamh na nDeachúna

Ar phár a tháinig slán chugainn ón mbliain
D'aois ár dTiarna míle dhá chéad ochtó, taispeántar
Gur sheol Eaglais Lochlannach na Graonlainne
Deachúna Crosáide go dtí Pápa na Róimhe
I riocht míle ceithre chéad seachtó punt éibhir
De starrfhiacla céad nócha is a haon bhálrus
A ghnóthaigh fiche sé phunt d'airgead geal glan.

Nár dheachúna iad san! Fiacla fada géara
Á stracadh as cloigne na rón is á seoladh
Ón dTuaisceart reoite go dtí an tOirthear loiscneach,
Fiacla geala Críostaí ag réabadh doircheacht Ioslaim,
Fiacla dragúin á gcur sa ghaineamh, ag síolrú
Fómhar fola atá fós á bhaint, deachúna
Á n-íoc agus á n-aisíoc arís ina milliúnta!

Reckoning the Tithes

A parchment that has been handed down to us
From the year of Our Lord twelve hundred and eighty,
Recounts that the Norse Church of Greenland
Sent Crusade Tithes to the Pope of Rome
In the form of one thousand four hundred and seventy pounds
Of ivory from the tusks of one hundred and ninety-eight walrus
Which realised twenty-six pounds of bright sterling silver.

Was not that some tithing! Long sharp teeth
Torn from the walrus heads and dispatched
From the frozen North to the burning East,
Bright Christian teeth ripping the darkness of Islam,
Dragons' teeth sown in the desert, seeding
A bloody harvest still being reaped, tithes
Being paid and repaid again in their millions!

III

Forógra Cásca

A Dhia is a ghlúinte
Mharfacha na marbh,
Leig dínn. Éirígí
Aníos ónár nguailne
Leis an bhfiach dubh a bhrúigh
Sibh orainn. Leig dúinn
Bheith sinn féin gan bheith
De shíor in bhur bhfiacha-se.
Imígí ag cabaireacht
Le fiacha san uaigneas;
Imígí go dtí an fásach
Ag séideadh bhur dtrumpaí.

Easter Proclamation

In the name of God and the deadly
Dead generations,
Enough is enough.
Get off our backs,
Together with the bird of death
You willed on us. Leave us
To be ourselves, without
Your debts clawing at our shoulders.
Take yourselves cawing
With ravens in the wilderness.
Take yourselves to the desert
To give free range to your blaring trumpets.

Sos Cogaidh, Nollaig 1914

Oíche chiúin, oíche
Chomh eadarthráthach sin
Gur ar éigin go gcloisfeá
An saol mór ag siosarnach
Slán leis an uile.

Oíche chiúin, oíche
Chomh mór as a riocht
Le riachtanaisí an ama
Gur ar éigean go mbeidh
A leithéid ann arís.

Truce, Christmas 1914

Silent night, the night
So deeply liminal
You would barely hear
The wide world whispering
Goodbye to all that.

Silent night, the night
So wrenched out of shape
By the time's imperatives
That its kind is unlikely
Ever again to be.

Mar a Chualathas ar an nGrinneall

*i gcuimhne chriú an fhomhuireáin Kursk, a fuair bás am éigin
mí Lúnasa 2000*

Giorraisc na focail iad, *Kursk* agus *Murmansk*.
Caithfear iad a chlaochló ... claochló ... claochló ...

Is cinnte gur tharla seo agus gur tharla siúd.
Níltear in aon amhras ... amhras ... amhras ...

Tá cluas ar an dtír le h-éisteacht.
Meastar go gcualathas cnag ... cnag ... cnag ...

Tá an tUachtarán ar saoire ag an bpointe seo.
Ní cheaptar é bheith oiriú... riú ... riú ...

Tá *politik* na tragóide seo thar a bheith *real*.
Caithfidh daoine a thuis ... a thuis ... a thuis...

Tá rúndacht i gceist, agus mórtas cine.
Nuair is gá, lorgófar cabhair ... cabhair ... cabhair ...

Tá póicín aeir fanta idir an dá dhoras, díreach
Ar an dtaobh thall ... taobh thall ... taobh thall ...

Cé go mbraithimid folús sa tsaol fo thoinn,
Níl aon cheist uisce faoi thalamh ... thalamh ... thalamh ...

Le teann ár mbróid, coimeádfar a gcuimhne
Buan go deo na ndeor ... na ndeor ... na ndeor ...

Níl aon fhianaise ann fós na gathanna cogaidh
Bheith ag sileadh nimhe ... sileadh nimhe ... sileadh nimhe ...

Má ardaítear na corpanna, cuirfear iad
Lena muintir, soir-siar ... soir-siar ... soir-siar ...

166

As Was Heard on the Seabed

in memory of the crew of the submarine Kursk, who died some time in August 2000

They're clipped, abrupt, those words *Kursk* and *Murmansk*.
They must be transformed ... transformed... transformed ...

It has been confirmed that such and such may have happened.
There is absolutely no doubt ... no doubt ... no doubt ...

The whole country is listening.
Knocking may have been heard ... been heard ... been heard ...

The President is on holidays at this point in time.
It is not deemed appropriate ... appropriate ... appropriate ....

The *politik* of this tragedy is more than *real*.
The people must understand ... understand ... understand ....

There are security issues, and national pride.
If necessary, help will be sought ... be sought ... be sought ...

There is a pocket of air between two bulkheads, just
On the other side ... other side ... other side ...

Although there are lacunae in underwater legislation
There is no question of conspiracy ... conspiracy ... conspiracy ....

Inspired by our pride in them, their memory will be kept
Cherished until the very end of time ... of time ... of time ...

There is as of now no evidence that any of the missiles
Are leaking toxic ... leaking toxic ... leaking toxic ...

If the bodies are recovered, they will be interred
With their people, lying east-west ... east-west ... east-west ...

Béasa an Bhroic

Ní hionmhuin leis an ríbhroc aoibhneas, aiteas, ná spórt,
Ni hionmhuin leo saoi, draoi, ná cumadóir ceoil.
– Séamus Dall Mac Cuarta

Ní thaobhaíonn an broc lucht éigse nó fíona
    Ar fhaitíos go lasfaí lóchrann ina phluais gan chead.

Tá sé scannraithe beo roimh solas na péintéireachta
    Mar go nochtann sí a leimhe is a léithe os comhair cháich.

Dá ainneoin féin, éistfidh sé anois is arís le amhrán
    Má tá na focail simplí, is de ghlanmheabhair ag gach éinne.

Taithíonn sé pluaiseanna a thaithigh a sheacht shinsear
    Ar eagla a chaillte i bpasáistí nárbh eol dá shrón.

Níl eagla ar roimh madraí agus fir ag teacht ist'oíche
    Ach roimh gáire na mban ag teacht is imeacht ón dtobar.

Má bhíonn amhras ar an bhfeirmeoir faoi thinneas a thréada
    Cuireann an aghaidh fidil an dubh ina gheal air.

Smaoinigh nach gá dó marachtaint faoin dtalamh
    Aimsíonn sé doircheacht agus é i lár an aonaigh.

Badger

Badger hates celebration, merrymaking, sport,
Abominates wits, wise men, music makers, poets.
  – Séamus Dall Mac Cuarta

Badger likes not those who like wine or poetry
   For fear an unauthorised torch might illuminate his tunnel.

Badger is terrified of the light that painters are familiar with
   Because it might expose his ghastliness to the world.

In spite of himself, Badger listens now and again to a song
   Provided the words are simple, and everyone has them by heart.

Badger frequents only passageways frequented by his predecessors
   For fear of being lost in places whose smell he does not know.

It is not the approach of hounds and men by night that Badger fears
   But the laughter of the women coming and going from the well.

If the farmer is uneasy because of sudden illness among his cattle
   The black and white mask makes light of all of his doubts.

Remember above all that there is no need to live underground.
   Badger can sniff out darkness in the heart of a fairground gathering.

Gáirleog

Chuireas na hiongna inniu,
Ag tumadh a ngile
Préamh faoi sa chré dubh.

Tráth chasadh na bliana
Nach shin buille
Tréan ar son an tsolais!

Garlic

I planted the cloves today,
Plunging their brightness
Root down in the black clay.

Now at the year's turning
Was not that indeed a mighty
Blow on the side of light!

Athphósadh ar Oileán Diúra

Gealgháireach i measc clocha an chladaigh
A chonac uaim é, sliogán muirín
Á leathadh féin faoin ngrian

Ag barra taoide, agus aoibh air
Mar a bheadh sé ag maíomh gur rug sé
Baindia an Ghrá i dtír in athuair.

Agus mar gur rugais barr gean ó Bhéanas deas
Thíolacas duit é, agus le fáinne geal
Na farraige mórthimpeall orainn,

Phósamar in athuair ar Oileán Diúra,
Sinn ag feitheamh ar bhád farantóireachta
Go hoileán ar oileán ag síneadh i ndiaidh a chéile.

Remarriage on the Isle of Jura

Radiant on the shingle stones
I spotted it first, a scallop-shell
Stretching itself under the sun

At high tide, beaming
With delight at having conveyed
The Goddess of Love ashore again.

And since you still outshine sweet Venus,
I tendered it to you, and with the bright ring
Of the surrounding sea encircling us,

We married again on the Isle of Jura,
As we waited to be ferried to island upon
Island surpassing itself in the distance.

Geit Áthais ar Oileán Bharra

Gíoscán doras Chill Bharra, agus an solas
Ag sileadh ar leacacha mhórchúiseacha
Na bhfear uasal, claíomh agus clogad
Greanta san ord agus san eagar cheart,
Giolla na haimsire á bhfaire leis na cianta.

Agus taobh thiar díobh, ar altóir shimplí
Lonnrach le *Ronseal*, i measc sliogán na trá,
Pósae ó *Herbarium*, crosóga tuí
Agus líníocht páistí, b'shiúd Bríd Chill Dara,
A súile dírithe in airde ar na frathacha,
Ar an tuáille *chainstore*, an líon *monofilament*
A bhí lonnaithe ansin fúthu go himpíoch,
Beag beann ar ghinealach is ar sheandacht.

Ag tiomáint thar nais dom go dtí an lóistín,
M'aigne ag spaisteoireacht, b'shiúd thíos iad
Ar roisín gainimhe ag gobadh amach
I mbarra taoide, iad tirim ar éigin:
Ealta roilleach, giollaí Bhríde,
A gclúmh dubh agus bán ina shailm
Peannaireachta ar an ngaineamh,
Fáinne a súl ar bís chun sliogán,
Agus a ngob fada dearg le gaoith.

D'fhanas scathaimhín á bhfaire,
Ag cuartú focail ar bith a chuimseodh
An *serendipity* a bhí le brath ar muir
Ar spéir is ar talamh. De gheit,
Do phíob mo chroí, agus d'eitil.

Surprised by Joy on the Isle of Barra

The door of Cill Bharra creaked and the light
Spilled onto the imposing grave-slabs
Of the aristocracy, sword and helmet
Engraved in correct rank and precedence,
The weather their squire through the ages.

And behind them, on a simple altar
Glowing with *Ronseal*, among the seashells,
A posy from *Herbarium*, straw crosses
And children's drawings, there was Brigid of Kildare,
Eyes lifted to the roof-beams.
On the chainstore towel, a monofilament net
Set imploringly below her,
Oblivious of lineage and antiquity.

As I drove to the B&B, my mind
All over the place – there below!
On a small spit of sand reaching out
Into the high tide, barely dry:
A flock of oystercatchers, Brigid's birds,
Their black and white plumage a psalm
Of calligraphy in the sand,
Their ringed eyes eager for shellfish,
Long red beaks set into the wind.

I stayed awhile watching them,
Sifting for a word to encompass
The serendipity that infused the air
And land and water. All at once,
My heart piped up, and away it flew.

Surprised by Joy ...

Ní féidir liom fós tiomáint thar abhainn
In Áth Dara, gan *Slán Le Máighe*
A chloisint á ardú go cúthaileach agat,
Mar gurbh caor, craobh agus cuach
Ba dhual i gcónaí duit agus dúchas
Seachas loime agus faobhracht na farraige
A thaobhaíos féin níos minice.

Agus fós tar éis seacht mbliain, iompaím
Le geit iontais seabhac a fheiscint
Croctha gan bogadh os cionn faille,
Na gloiní íslithe agam od lorg
Chun creathadh ar éigin sin na sciathán
A rianú agus a roinnt leat.

Agus go leor eile: an fál nua ag tabhairt fothaine,
Na bláthanna móinéir a chuireas ag fás go rábach anois,
Teacht is imeacht páistí, tráchtas a scríobhas,
Dánta a foilsíodh, leabhair le foilsiú,
Clingireacht na dtréad cois locha sa tSlóibhéin,
An solas ag sileadh trín duilliúr ar an sliabh.

Agus éist! Tá rón ag ceol amuigh ar Charraig Éanna.
Ach táir gluaiste intíre, i bhfad siar thar abhainn.

Surprised by Joy …

Still I cannot drive across the bridge
In Adare, without hearing the tentative
Notes of you rising up *Slán Le Máighe*
Because it was berry, branch and bird
That were ever in your birth and breeding
More than the bare and edgy seashore
That was the haunt I favoured.

And still after seven years I turn around
Abruptly, all agog to see a hawk
Hung unstirring above the cliff-edge,
My binoculars lowered to find you
So that I can show and trace and share
The curves of those barely trembling wings.

And so much more: a new hedge for shelter,
Those meadow flowers I'm trying out,
The kids coming and going, my dissertation,
Poems published, books to be published,
The tinkling of lakeside cattle-bells in Slovenia,
Light slanting through foliage on a mountainside.

And listen! A seal is singing out on Carraig Éanna.
But you've gone inland now, far beyond the river.

Marbhna Oisín

i.m. Oisín O'Mahony, naíonán

Mar gur ar éigean ar shroich tú Tír na nÓg
Sular sciobadh arís siar thar farraige thú
Mar nár thuigis riamh draíocht na dúthaí sin
Ná fós arís a bheith dá ceal
Mar ná rabhais riamh faoi gheasa chinn óir
Ná aon chapall bhán faoi smacht na lámha agat
Mar nach raibh agat aon agallamh le seanóirí
Ná seanchas peile, ná camán id lámh agat
Mar gur robáladh an taisce a shamhlaigh d'athair duit
Agus aisling gheal do mháthar
Is id dhiaidhse atáthar, Oisín, is tá an saol ar fad
Titithe as a riocht, mar ghaiscíoch ón diallait.

Lament for Oisín

i.m. Oisín O'Mahony, infant

Because you had barely arrived at Tír na nÓg
Before you were swept back out to sea again;
Because you never realised the magic of that place
Nor yet again what it is to lose it;
Because you were never spellbound by golden hair
Nor held the reins of a white horse in your hands;
Because you had never conversed with old men,
Never talked football, nor gripped a hurley;
Because your father was robbed of the treasure he imagined,
And your mother of her brightest dreaming;
We are forlorn, Oisín, and the whole world
Has tumbled to the ground, like a hero from the saddle.

Ar Chósta Malabar

do Ghabriel, le buíochas

Agus chonac gur thángadar go dtí an bruach
Sa chóntráth agus teas an lae ag maolú,
Mná stádmhara na gcailleacha fada dubha
Ag taibhsiú go ciúin ina nduine is ina nduine
Ina seasamh le hais a chéile ag barra taoide
Gur dhein aon líne amháin dorcha fad na trá
Fad líne chúrach na toinne a thagann ina suaill
I bhfad aniar chun briseadh ar chósta Malabar.

Chonac páistí leo agus ógánaigh le heitleoga
Ar cleitearnach i mbéal na gaoithe, leoithne sáile
Á gcorraí, is ag muirniú freisin éadan na mban,
A gceann tógtha, ar bís chun na cumhrachta.
Agus ardaíodh leis sin dordán amhránaíochta
Ar foluain os cionn an tslua, ar nós ealta focal
Ag cantaireacht faoi cheilt, na mná ag stánadh
Amach thar luí na gréine, siar i dtreo na hAráibe.

On the Coast of Malabar

for Gabriel, with gratitude

And I saw that they came to the shore
At dusk as the day's heat was easing,
Women stately in their long dark robes
Approaching one after the silent other
To stand close along the high tide mark
Until they formed a single line on the beach
The length of a breaking wave that had swelled
From the far west to the coast of Malabar.

I saw children too, and teenagers with kites
Fluttering in the wind's mouth, that salt breeze
Stirring them, and caressing the women's brows,
Their uplifted heads eager for the fragrance.
And gradually a humming rose from the crowd
To circle overhead, as if it were a flock of words
Chanted from a secret place, the women staring
Far beyond the sunset, westward towards Arabia.

Paidir Oíche

do Shiobhán Ní Fhoghlú

Gabhaim buíochas as an lá míorúilteach seo atáim díreach tar éis a
  chaitheamh
Mar ar maidin chuas ag rith ar an dtrá (ag m'aois-se) agus d'éirigh liom,
Cé go rabhas mall, rith tríd na scamaill – na scáileanna tá's agat a
  chíonn tú
Ar an ngaineamh fliuch díreach ar imeall na taoide – agus níor thiteas.

Agus dheineas anraith, go leor don lá inniu agus cion ceithre lá
  eile sa reoiteoir,
Agus thirimíos dhá líne níocháin, agus i measc cleitearnach agus
  slapar
Na mbraitlíní rith línte anseo is ansiúd liom agus scríobhas agus
  chlóscríobhas
An dán tráthnóna – ní hé an ceann seo é – agus táim sásta leis, is
  dóigh liom.

Agus anois díreach sa choimheascar chualas don gcéad uair i
  mbliana an chuach
Agus cé gurbh im chluais chlé ar mhí-ámharaí an tsaoil a chuala í,
  do chasas
Deiseal ar an dtoirt (agus ar ámharaí an tsaoil) agus tríd is tríd
  táim meáite
Go mbeidh rath ar an mbliain agus ormsa agus ar ghach aon
  neach faoin spéir.

Night Prayer

for Siobhán Ní Fhoghlú

I offer up thanks for the miraculous day I have just passed
Because this morning I ran on the beach (at my age) and
    succeeded,
Although I was slow, in running through the clouds – you know,
    the reflections
On the wet sand just at the edge of the tide – and I didn't fall.

And I made soup, enough for today and for four more days in the
    freezer,
And I dried two lines of washing, and between the flap and the
    flutter
Of the sheets a few lines came to me and I wrote and typed out
The poem this evening – I don't mean this one – and I'm happy
    with it, I think.

And just now in the twilight I heard, for the first time this year, a
    cuckoo
And although it was inauspiciously in my left ear that I heard it, I
    spun around
Clockwise on the spot (and auspiciously) so taking all things
    together, I'm determined
That the year will turn out well for me and for every single being
    under the sun.

IV

An Logainmneoir

do Bhreandán Ó Cíobháin

Stopann sé scathaimhín ag Carraig Coiscéim,
Ag meá rithim an uisce a scéitheann isteach
Agus amach de réir rúibricí na haimsire.

N'fheadar sé an guth na n-áitreabhóirí
Nó foghar na toinne, nó seanchas ar foluain
Fós ar an ngaoth a rug go dtí an ball seo é.

Ach tuigeann sé chomh tromchúiseach
Is atá an choiscéim seo, cé gur beag
Idir an charraig seo agus an charraig thall.

Tuigeann sé gur beag idir ainm is anam,
Gur mór idir friotal agus balbhacht,
Gur beag idir taobh tíre agus iontaobhas.

Tógann sé an choiscéim, coiscéim a fhágann
Lorg ar an aer. Cromann sé láithreach
Ar nótaí a bhreacadh dá leabhar athghabhála.

Toponomist

for Breandán Ó Cíobháin

He lingers for a space at Carraig Coiscéim,
Weighing the rhythm of the tide surging in
And out following the weather's rubric.

He doesn't know if it is the inhabitants' voice,
The utterances of the tide, or folklore floating
Still in the air that brought him here.

But he knows full well just how essential
This footstep is, although there's little between
This rock over here and that rock over there.

He knows there is little between naming and animating,
That there is much between articulation and silence,
That there is little between landscape and inscape.

He takes the footstep, a footstep that leaves
An imprint on the air. There and then he begins
To jot down notes for his book of repossession.

Coiscéim Aimhirghin

Agus a chos dheis á leagan ar an dtalamh aige, dúirt Aimhirghin:
Mé gaoth ar muir
Mé tonn díleann
Mé glór mara
Mé damh seacht gcomhrac
Me fiolar ar fhaill
Mé deor drúchta faoin ngréin
Me áilleacht fáis
Mé torc ar ghail
Me bradán sa linn
Mé loch ar mhá
Mé suí eagna
Mé ga faoi bhua ag slaí sa chath
Mé dia a adhnann tine sa cheann

    Cé a dheineann réidh clochán sléibhe?
    Cé a chaitheann solas ar chruthanna na gealaí?
    Cé fhógraíonn cá luífidh an ghrian?
    Cé a threoraíonn tonnta réaltacha mar bha na mara?
    Cé air a shoilsíonn na tonnta réaltacha sin?
    Cen dream, cén dia a chuireann faobhar ar lanna i ndún ailse?
    Caoineadh na nga. Caoineadh na gaoithe.

The Amergin Step

Setting his right foot on the land, Amergin said:
Am wind on sea
Am wave swelling
Am ocean's voice
Am stag of seven clashes
Am falcon on cliff
Am sunlit dewdrop
Am rarest of herbs
Am boar enraged
Am salmon in pool
Am lake in plain
Am learning's essence
Am sharpened spear dealing death
Am god who kindles fire in the head.

Who makes smooth the stony mountain?
Who elucidates the lives of the moon?
Who proclaims where the sun will rest?
Who leads starlit waves like cattle from the ocean?
On whom do those starlit waves smile?
What troop, what god edges blades in a plague-struck fortress?
Keening of weapons. Keening of wind.

Freagra Scéine ar Aimhirghin

Más tusa gaoth na mara
    Is mé an fharraige om shearradh féin faoid leoithne
Más tonn díleann thú
    Is sliogán folamh mé ag tnúth led theacht
Más tú gáir na stoirme
    Is mé lapadaíl na taoide i mbrothall nóna
Más damh seacht gcomhrac thú
    Tiocfad go mánla chugat ar aiteann
Más seabhac thú ar an bhfaill
    Beannód thú le liricí fuiseogacha
Más deoir drúchta faoin ngréin thú
    Brúfad féar na maidne leat
Más tú is áille a fhásann
    Bláthód leat bliain ar bhliain
Más torc ar mire thú
    Cuirfead geasa gháire ar na fiacla fada agat
Más bradán thú sa linn
    Meallfad cuileoga ina gcéadta chugat
Más loch ar mhá thú
    Raghad go tóin poill ionat
Más tú rún na héigse
    Mise na naoi mBéithe agat
Má bhíonn faobhar ort chun troda
    Cuirfead ceangal na ceanúlachta ort
Má bhíonn tinfeadh á adhaint sa cheann agat
    Séidfead síol na tine duit

Tá fhios ag mo chroí istigh cé réitigh an bealach dom,
Cé ba réalt eolais, cé bhronn grian agus gealach orm,
Is in ainneoin na gcloch seo, agus an solas ag dul in éag,
Mairfead scáth ar scáth leat, focal ar fhocal leis an ngaoth.

ag uaigh Scéine, 21 Nollaig 1999

Scéine's Reply to Amergin

If you are the wind on the sea
   I am the water tingling under your breeze.
If you are a wave in flood
   I am an empty shell dreaming of your coming.
If you are the roar of a storm
   I am the tide lapping in the noon heat.
If you are the stag of seven horns
   I will pick my way to you gracefully through furze.
If you are a hawk on the cliff
   I will bless you with lyrics of larksong.
If you are a dewdrop in the sun
   I will bruise the morning grass with you.
If you are the fairest of flowers
   I will blossom year upon year with you.
If you are a maddened boar
   I will charm your tusks into laughter.
If you are a salmon in the pool
   I will lure infinities of insects to you.
If you are a lake in the plain
   I will plumb your very depths.
If you are the essence of poetry
   I am all of your muses.
If you are edging towards a fight
   I will bewitch you to bluntness.
If you are kindling inspiration in the mind
   I will blow on the seed of the fire for you.

I know in my heart who made the way smooth for me,
Was a star of knowledge for me, gave the sun and moon to me,
And though the stones close in, and light moves towards its end,
We will shadow one another, word for word with the wind.

21 December 1999, at the grave of Scéine

Labhrann Érannán

Mise i dtosach a chonaic, naoi dtonn amach,
Crochta in airde ar chrann seoil na loinge,
An tír mar thairngireacht romham ós cionn an cheo.
Ach ba ag an neomat gur scaoileas uaim an gháir

Gur ghabh creathán grod ó thosach deireadh na cíle,
Gur bhris an crann, gur caitheadh siar amach
Ar chúl mo chinn ar an gcarraig mé, gur slogadh
Isteach sa tsáile mé, gur idirshaolaíodh mé

Im neach farraige ar charraig cois cósta,
Im aonarán féachana, im aonarán éisteachta
Ag an dul i dtír agus ag gach a d'eascair as:
Deasghnátha, tithe agus glór páistí ar an dtrá.

Chuala uaim iad, an bád ag siosarnach
Suas ar an ngaineamh, an liú caithréimeach,
Torann na rámha á dtarraingt ar bord,
An fuadar chun chladaigh, agus focla tromchúiseacha

Mo dhearthár ag scaothaireacht leis gurbh é
Féin an ghaoth, féin an seabhach, féin an bradán,
Féin an uile ní beo ar bith, agus neamhbheo
Siúd ná mairfeadh trí lá ar an gcarraig seo,

Le báirnigh á scríobadh, faoileáin á chiapadh,
Agus gan ach cleasaíocht focal mar scáth aige
Seachas dúire sin na carraige atá anois buanaithe
Go docht im aigne. Mar is gá dom. Mar is fuath liom.

Tonn i ndiaidh toinne om bhascadh, om thachtadh
Le cúr mire mar a bheadh bainne cíche na Baidhbhe,

Érannán Speaks

It was I who first saw it, over nine waves
From my perch high in the rigging,
The land like a prophecy over the mast.
But it was on the very instant I yelled out

That the keel shook from stem to stern,
The mast split, I was flung out
On my head on the rock, was swallowed
Back into the saltwater, was otherworlded

Into a sea-being on an offshore rock,
A lone witness, a lone listener
To the landing and to all that ensued:
Ceremonies, houses and children's voices on the beach.

I heard it from a distance, the boats whispering
Up onto the sand, the great fanfaronade,
The clamorous shipping of the oars,
The scramble onto shingle, and the ponderous words

Of my brother windbagging that he himself
Was wind and wave, was hawk and salmon,
Was all being that lived, and did not –
Himself who wouldn't last three days on this rock,

Harrowed by limpets, tormented by gulls,
With only the trickery of words to shelter him
Instead of the rocky stubbornness now calcified
Firmly into my soul. My essence. My hate.

Wave after wave battering me, choking me
With crazed foam like the breast milk of the Fury,

Om bheathú chun báis, is an fheamainn ghoirt
Om lascadh gan staonadh chun beatha arís.

Mhaíodar gur cuireadh thall mé, le Scéine,
Ansiúd ar an gcnoc, faoi chlocha arda
Chun mé a threorú chun gealaigh agus gréine
Maíomh chomh folamh leis an uaigh féin.

Conas a chuirfí nach raibh ann le cur?
Mo chorp i smidiríní spéire agus farraige,
Gan chliabhán, gan uaigh, scoite amach ar charraig
Idir chósta mo dhúchais agus cósta mo mhéine.

Níor leagas mo chos ar thalamh úr, níor chanas
Aon fhocal a mhaireann, níor ghabhas seilbh
Ar aon dúthaigh, níor luadh aon scéal liom
Ach mar a bheadh iarmhír ann, nó as.

Táim níos faide siar ná cuimhne na ndaoine,
Ann ar éigin ar Charraig Éanna. Ach éist:
Tá mianach sa charraig, lá i ndiaidh lae,
Ná faightear sa bhfoclaíocht is buaine ar bith.

Nurturing death in me, then the bitter seaweed
Whipping me relentlessly to life again.

They claimed I was buried there with Scéine,
Over there on the hill, under standing stones
To direct me towards the sun and the moon –
A claim as vain and empty as the grave itself.

How can you bury what is not there to be buried?
My body fragmented into sea and sky,
Without cradle, without grave, outcast on a rock
Between my native shore and the shore of my longing.

I did not set foot on new land, did not sing
Words that lasted, did not appropriate
Any territory, played no part in stories
But as an afterword, neither here nor there.

I go back farther than race memories,
Barely here on Carraig Éanna. But listen:
There is mettle in the rock, day after day,
Not found in the longest of long-lasting words.

Labhrann Donn

Is mé dorchadas m'ainm féinig,
An taobh thall den ngealach,
Deireadh báire na gile,
Tóin an mhála fáiscithe.
Is mé a mhúchann an dé deiridh.

Formad le mo dheártháir, adúradar,
A tharraing mí-ádh orainn araon,
Sea, agus cíochras míchuíosach chun troda
Ba chúis nár roinneadh Éire liom.
Bladar. Fuath do ghach aon neach beo
Agus cíochras chun féasta na gcnuimh
Is bun le mo ríocht. Agus féach!
Éire gan roinnt ag triall ar mo thigh-se.

Donn Dumhach. Teach Duinn.
Níl cion ar ainm an oileáin.
Luaitear tarbh liom, bó agus lao faram.
Bídís ag iníor tamall.

Ní thagann iascairí im ghaobhar
Ar eagla a slogtha scun scan
Ins na roithleáin timpeall orm.
Ach tá traimilí foighne agam,
Agus línte ná briseann.

Tá tigh solais ar an oileán
Agus dord a fhógraíonn ceo.
Ach slogaimse díodar gach solais
Agus sním mar cheo trí phollairí na marbh.

Donn Speaks

I am the darkness of my own name,
The far side of the moon,
The final end of brightness,
The narrowing *cul de sac*.
It is I who chokes off the last breath.

Envy of my brother, they said,
Brought bad luck to both of us,
Yes, and an inordinate bloodthirst
Meant no part of Ireland was for me.
Bullshit. Hatred towards all living beings
And a thirst for the feasting of worms
Is my right of kingship. And look!
The whole of Ireland travels towards my house.

Donn of the Dunes. Donn's House.
The name of the island is not liked.
I am known as a bull. The cow and calf are close.
Let them graze awhile.

Fisherman don't approach me
For fear they'd be swallowed whole
In the maelstrom around me.
But I have trammels of patience
And cords that will not break.

There is a lighthouse on the island
And a horn that trumpets fog.
But I swallow the dregs of all light
And I flow like a mist through the nostrils of the dead.

Tá mo chapall cloiste agat
Go doimhin san oíche. Téanam go luath
Ag marcaíocht ar na dumhacha.

You have heard my horses
In the dead of the night. Come with me soon
To ride on the dunes.

Díthreabhach, Drom Caor

Ní bhfaightear do thuairisc
I gcruas na cloiche,
Ná sa bhfoirfeacht gan ainm
Atá in ealaín do chroise.

Ach chítear do bheannacht
A bhí faoi cheilt insa gcaonach,
Ina bhoige is ina ghlaise
Faoi dhealán obann gréine.

Agus fógraítear morthimpeall
Nach bhfuilir id aonar,
I gceiliúireadh na mbeach
Is an éanlaith ag glaoch ort.

Hermit, Dromkeare

You are not found ingrained
In this hardness of stone
Or the anonymous art
Chiselled on your cross.

But your blessing emerges
From its nest in the moss,
Tendering green softness
In a sudden gleam of sun.

And the air is insistent
That you're not alone here
As bees concelebrate
And birdsong invokes you.

An Géarchaoineadh, Sceilg Mhichíl

do Mhícheál Ua Ciarmhaic

Bean An Uaill a luaitear liom go minic. N'fheadar.
Táim chomh fada sin cromtha im charraig
Ná cuimhin liom bheith baineann ná fireann,
Ná feadar an caointeoireacht fir nó caointeoireacht mná
A bhíonn anois agam, nó a bhí ariamh agam..
Caointeoireacht chloiche, seachas aon rud eile.
Seachtarach do gach aon rud eile. Scoite.

Táim ag caoineadh réabadh na carraige,
An chloch chruaidh scoiltithe uaithi féin,
Na leaca a leagadh ina gcéimeanna,
Á gcasúiriú chun cruiceogachta, á smachtú
Ag clingireacht clog, ag crónán paidreacha.
Táim ag caoineadh na carraige ina smionagar
Ag púdar buile innealltóirí, failltreacha
Brúite, briste chun bóthair, chun tí solais.
Táim ag caoineadh mo dhíothú féin,
Mé athmhúnluithe ag oilithrigh is ag aimsir.

Tá mo dhá lámh sínte romham amach
Agus uaireanta tagann éanacha chugam,
Ag déanamh, mar dhea, neamhshuim díom
Is de mo dhúire, a súile is a gclúmh
Ar bís chun aeir agus chun solais.
Ach tagann siad fós ag tuirlingt orm
Faoi mar ba naomh mé i seanscéal,
Mar a bheidís faoi gheasa ag mo chaoineadh.

Tá Críost a chaoineadh agam, mar adeir siad,
In éineacht le mná caointe Iérúsaileim.

The Wailing Woman, Skellig Michael

for Mícheál Ua Ciarmhaic

The Wailing Woman, they mostly call me. I don't know.
I am so long bent over into stone
That I don't remember being man or woman,
I don't know if it's a man's keening or a woman's
I make now, or ever made.
A stone keening, more than all else.
External to all else. Alien.

I wail for the rupturing of the rock,
The adamant rock splintered from itself,
The slabs being set into steps,
Hammered into beehive huts, dominated
By tinkling bells, the drone of prayer.
I mourn the rock in smithereens
By the crazed powder of engineers, cliffs
Battered and bruised into a road, a lighthouse.
I am wailing for my own uprooting,
My transformation by pilgrims and the weather.

My hands are spread out before me
And sometimes birds come to me,
Pretending to ignore me,
Ignore my hardness, their eyes and plumage
Eager for air and for light.
But they still come to land on me,
As if I were a sainted legend,
As if they're in thrall to my wailing.

I wail for Christ, as is rightly said,
With the wailing women of Jerusalem.

Ach táim ag caoineadh freisin na mná caointe
Ar fad, thoir, thiar, thuaidh agus theas,
Lámh spréite acu chun cheamara, lámh eile
Ag dáileadh bratacha ar ógánaigh.
Táim ag caoineadh na gcaointeoirí
Is iad ag ceiliúradh na caointeoireachta abú.

Táim ag caoineadh glúinte gonta na noilithreach
A ghabh tharam ag siosarnach píonóis.
Táim ag caoineadh mo bhodhaire féin dá bpaidreacha,
Is a mbodhaire siúd do hósanna an aeir ina dtimpeall.

Táim cromtha faoi ualach na gealaí,
Faoina reoiteacht; faoina séanadh
Mí i ndiaidh míosa, rabharta i ndiadh rabharta,
Gurb í mo mháthair í agus máthair na farraige,
Gurb í tuile agus trá, dá hainneoin féin.

Ach umhlaím gach maidin roimh ghealadh an lae
Anoir chugam ón mhórthír, mo dhrom
Go diongabháilte le dul faoi na gréine,
Mar gur mó liom soineantacht an tsolais ar maidin
Ná ciall cheannaigh an dorchadais i ndeireadh an lae.
Agus coinneod m'aghaidh mar fhuinneog altóra
Chun an oirthir, ag súil le fuipíní áiféiseacha
Ag filleadh arís is arís le gobanna ioldaite lán éisc.

But I wail also for the wailing women
Everywhere, east, west, north and south,
One arm spread to the camera, the other
Distributing flags to the young.
I mourn for the mourners
Who celebrate the mourning.

I mourn for the raw knees of pilgrims
Who pass by me whispering punishment,
I mourn my deafness to their prayers
And their deafness to the hosanna of the surrounding air.

I am bent under the weight of the moon,
Her iciness; of her denial,
Month after month, tide after spring tide,
That she is my mother and the sea's mother,
That she is, in spite of herself, the flow and the ebb.

But I bow each morning before the dawn
Rising to me from the mainland, my back
Resolutely to the setting sun,
For I value the innocence of morning light
More than the dearly bought knowledge of evening darkness.
And I will keep my face like an altar window
To the east, waiting for ludicrous puffins
Coming again and again with multicoloured, fish-brimming beaks.

Eadarlúid Oíche Gaoithe

Ar sos siúlóide ón bpeannaireacht
Beirim ar thigh solais na Sceilge
Idir scamaill agus réaltanna
Ag uainíocht gaetha fada fuarchúiseacha
Ar thigh solais Oileán Doinn ó dheas.

Samhlaím Ir agus Donn ina mbun,
Cuimhní goirte sáile ag crá na beirte,
Iad ag breacadh cóid rúnda solais
Idir a chéile oileánacha, dréachtanna seifte
Don athscríobh, don Leabhar Nua Gabhála.

Interval on a Windy Night

Strolling, on a break from writing,
I catch the Skellig lighthouse
Between clouds and stars
Alternating long, calculating beams
With the lighthouse on the Bull to the south.

I sense Ir and Donn behind all this,
Both tormented by bitter, salty memories,
Swapping secret coded messages
Between their islanded selves, draft plans
For the rewrite, for the New Book of Invasions.

Oileánú

Tá an Sceilg iata ag an aimsir.
Gaoth ag éirí arís. Grian agus scamaill
In iomarbhá airgid agus luaidhe
Go geal éatrom, go dubh trom, fuadar
Agus fuirse faoin bhfarraige atá meáite
Ar oilean i ndiaidh oileain aonair
A chruthú ar dhromchla na cruinne.

Ní ann do Uíbh Ráthach ná do Bhéarra.
Ar fhíor na spéire, chím, ar éigin,
An Scairbh, Duibhinis, Oileán Dá Cheann
Ag síneadh uaim, smeadar i ndiaidh smeadair,
Ó dheas isteach sa gceo, amach san aimsir.
Mar sheilimide éigin farraige, cúngaím isteach
Ionam féin, im pheann luaidhe, insan oileán.

Islanding

Skellig is enclosed by the weather.
Wind rising again. Sunlight and clouds
In a silver and lead contest
Of airy light and heavy dark, a hustle
And bustle driving a sea that's determined
To create island after solitary island
All over the surface of the world.

Iveragh and Beara have disappeared.
On the horizon, I make out, just,
Scariff, Deenish, Two Head Island,
Stretching from me, smudge after smudge,
Southward into the fog, out into the weather.
Like some sea-snail or other, I shrink
Into myself, into my pencil, into the island.

Reic na Sceilge

Sceilg Mhichíl ar reic is ar díol
Trí chamastaíl ghiollaí an stáit seo,
A chúlaigh go rúnda ó chúram an dúchais
Ar son scillingí suaracha *Star Wars*.

Lúnasa 2014

Skellig a Rock-bottom Deal

Sceilg Mhichíl's just a rock-bottom deal
Through the devious schemes of its guardians
Retreating in secret from their vow of safekeeping
For the miserable shillings of *Star Wars*.

August, 2014

Cailleach Chloiche Bhéarra

Tá tú préachta, a chréatúir,
Id staic chloiche i mBéarra,
Agus rian na gaoithe
Is na gréine greanta
I línte do chreimithe,
Rian na mblianta
Ins na ribí liatha
De dhuileascar na gcloch
Is folt duit anois,
D'aghaidh dírithe ar thrá
Agus tuile na farraige.

Tusa a mhaígh
Go mbítheá fite fuaite
Le ríthe buacha,
Tusa a thug dúshlán
Naomh agus cléireach,
Is ná tabharfá an t-éitheach
Do Mhac Dé féin
Bheith lúbtha id ghéaga,

Tusa go bhfuil rian do cholainne
Ainmnithe ar fud na dúthaí,
Cíoch anseo, cúm ansiúd,
Srón, fiacal agus folt
Fós od thuairisc, fós
Ag siosarnach scéil do scéil,

Tusa a dhein mórtas
As bronntanais ríthe,
Éadach fíneálta,
Capaill agus carbaid,

The Stone Woman of Beara

You're petrified, you poor thing,
Into a stone pillar in Beara,
The harrowing of the wind
And ravaging of the sun
Scored into your sides,
The passage of years
Dried into the grey strands
Of stony lichen
That cling to you,
Your face turned to the ebb
And flow of the tide.

You who boasted
Of being twined
Around triumphant kings,
You who defied
Saints and clerics,
You who would not shrink
From the Son of God himself
Being limb upon limb with you,

You whose shape and weight
Are named all over the land,
A breast here, a hollow there,
Nose, tooth, flowing hair
Still recalling you, still
Whispering rumours of sightings,

You who gloried
In the gifts of kings,
Silks and fine linens,
Horses, chariots,

Fíon den scoth,
Féach anois thú
I dtuilleamaí tabhartas
Ní ó rí ná aire
Ach ón gcosmhuintir
Ag gabháil thar bráid:
Pinginí meirgeacha
Á bhfágaint ag fámairí
I roicne do chraicne,
Sliogáin is coinnle
Á gceangal le chéile
Acu siúd atá ag lorg
Faoisimh ón gcathair,
Fraoch agus caonach
Fite fuaite in éineacht
Ag ógánaigh phéacacha
I bhfochar a chéile
I ngrianghraf gléineach.
Is ar mh'anam nach bhfuileadar
Ríonach agus ríoga!

Ach tusa, a chréatúir,
Anseo i mBéarra
Ag stánadh ar an bhfarraige
Le radharc na Caillí Béarra
Glan gléineach ar deireadh:
Tá do rabharta mhór ar deireadh tráite,
Ár ndála uile, gan súil le tuile.

And the rarest of wines,
Look at you now
Dependent on offerings,
Not from kings or ministers
But from commoners
Passing the way:
Rusting small change
Deposited by tourists
In the folds of your skin,
Shells and candles
Netted together
By those who seek
Sanctuary from the city,
Heather and moss
Plaited and twined
By golden lads and lasses
Wrapped around themselves
In a lucent photograph.
And are they not truly
Prince and princess!

But you, you poor thing,
Here in Beara
Staring at the sea,
Your fabled vision
Finally and perfectly clear:
Your spring tide has in the end
Ebbed, as all our tides, beyond return.

Ag Éisteacht Le Dord na nDamh

do Frank Lewis

Tá an ghrian ag suirí leis an ngeimhreadh sa ghleann
Agus glór ag teacht anall is abhus ar an aer,
Dord mór-is-fiú ag sní ó bheann go beann.

Idir sinn agus léas, faobhrach mar lann,
Féach an damh seacht mbeann greanta ar an spéir.
Tá an ghrian ag suirí leis an ngeimhreadh sa ghleann.

Éist bodhrán an dúlra á bhualadh le fonn,
Píobaireacht na n-éan ag freagairt dá réir
Agus dord mór-is-fiú ag sní ó bheann go beann.

Maireann dord sleá na Féinne i gcuimhne na gcrann
Atá rábach le duilliúr, le cnó is le caor.
Tá an ghrian ag suirí leis an ngeimhreadh sa ghleann.

An ceol is ceolmhaire amuigh, sin ceol gach ní atá ann.
Tá bithnóta ceoil anois á sheinm inár ngaobhar
Agus dord mór-is-fiú ag sní ó bheann go beann.

Tá an glór seo le cianta i scéal agus rann,
Is má chailltear an macalla, díolfar as go daor.
Tá an ghrian ag suirí leis an ngeimhreadh sa ghleann,
Agus dord mór-is-fiú ag sní ó bheann go beann.

Cill Áirne, Deireadh Fómhair 2003

Listening to the Roaring of the Stags

for Frank Lewis

The sun is making love to winter in the glen
And a voice can be heard echoing here and there,
An imperious ululation that rolls from ben to ben.

Between us and the light, sharp as a bladed edge,
See the seven-horned stag etched into the air.
The sun is making love to the winter in the glen.

The elemental drumming is more and more intense
As the piping of the birds becomes antiphonal prayer,
And that imperious ululation rolls from ben to ben.

The spear-wail of the Fianna lives on in branch and stem
With leaf and nut and berry in rampant display,
While the sun is making love to the winter in the glen.

The music of what happens is music without end
And a universal note now permeates the air,
An imperious ululation that rolls from ben to ben.

This voice has called through ages in story and in verse
And if we lose its echo, the loss will cost us dear.
The sun is making love to winter in the glen
And that imperious ululation rolls from ben to ben.

Killarney, October 2003

Seachrán Sí

do Phádraig Mac Fhearghusa

I lúb na coille
    Go doimhin san oíche,
Do gheal go léir
    Curtha ina dhubh ort,
Siosarnach na nduilleog
    Ag síorfhonóid fút,
Is tú i ndeargbhaol
    Imeacht le craobhacha,

Ní mór duit stad
    Díreach mar a bhfuilir,
Do cheann a chóiriú
    Bun os cionn,
Do shúile a dhíriú
    Droim ar ais,
Is an féin istigh
    A iompó glan amach.

A Fairy Floundering

for Pádraig Mac Fhearghusa

In the bend of the wood
    Deep in the night
All of your brightness
    Gulled into darkness
The whispering leaves
    A constant derision
Tempted to do a flyer
    Away with the birds,

You must stop dead
    Still where you are
Position your head
    Upside down
Direct your eyes
    Back to front
And turn your inner self
    Clean inside out.

Ceangailte

Tá an ceo ina shrathar fhada
Ag luascadh ar dhá thaobh
Drom an Bhlascaoid.

Beag beann ar ár leithéidí
Tá an t-oileán ag treabhadh leis
Ag iompar ualach na farraige.

Harnessed

The mist hangs and sways
Like turf-creels on either side
Of the Blasket's backbone.

Oblivious of the likes of us
The island ploughs on
Bearing the burden of the sea.

Bean Chrúite na Bó

Ag crú na bó a bhí an bhean, ar a sáimhín só
Mar a bhíodh, Domhnach is dálach, ar an stól,
An bhó ar éigin ag bogadh, ag tál
Go toilteanach faoi mhealladh na lámh
A raibh aithne aici orthu agus acu siúd
Uirthi, an chlingireacht sa bhuicéad mar cheol
A raibh sean chleachtadh ag an mbeirt air.

Le rithim na crúite agus solas an tráthnóna
Ag beannú di trín doras leath-oscailte,
As cúinne éigin dá cuimhne, dá seanchuimhne,
Tháinig rabhcán beag neafaiseach chuici, agus d'oscail
A béal agus chan. Thál an bhó léi, á tionlacan.

Líon an cró le ceol, an buicéad le bainne.

Bhuail clog go toll lasmuigh. Chuala sí
Guthannna, scáileanna ag dul thar bráid.
Chuir sí uaithi díomhaoine an amhráin.

Scoilt an tráthnóna le breithiúntas, agus chrónaigh.

Ghéaraigh aigne na mná. Ghéaraigh a lámha
Ar shiní na bó. Chorraigh an bhó cos mhíshuaimhneach.
Ghéaraigh an tráthnóna mar a ghéaródh bainne.

Woman Milking

The woman milked the cow, at her ease
As always, Sundays and weekdays, on the stool,
The cow barely stirring, yielding
Willingly to the persuasion of hands
She knew as well as they knew
Her, the tinkling in the bucket
Like music long familiar to the pair.

With the rhythm of milking and the evening light
Hailing her through the half-open door,
From some part of her memory, her old memory,
A few trivial verses came to her, and she opened
Her throat and sang. The cow yielded, accompanying her.

The byre filled with music, the bucket with milk.

A bell tolled somewhere outside. She heard
Voices, sensed shadowy figures passing.
She cast aside the idleness of the song.

The evening was riven with judgement, and darkened.

The woman's mind stiffened. Her hands stiffened
On the cow's teats. The cow stamped an uneasy hoof.
The evening soured, like tainted milk.

Labhrann an Chailleach

do Ghearóid Ó Crualaoich

Cé mise, cén scéal atá agamsa
Le h-insint ar na saolta seo, cén dán
Le reic feasta i mbéal na haimsire?
Cén t-amhrán a déarfar, cén scéal a inseofar
Ormsa amach anseo ach scéal scéil
A d'inseodh fiach is a shéanfadh feannóg?

Lorg coiscéime i mbaol a shlogtha
Sa gcaonach creathach ar bharr an bhogaigh.

Iomairí i dtaibhreamh cliotair is allais
Á searradh féin faoi dhearúdacht raithnigh.

Macalla ar fán i gcúlaibh na cuimhne
Mar a bheadh fead fiolair i ngob na gaoithe.

Tá an chré imithe le fada sa bhfraoch
Gan rian cos nó leagadh lámh uirthi
Le cuimhne leochailleach na ndaoine.
Níl fios mo chuid feasa ag cuisliú aníos
Trí lúth is trí féith go smior is go croí,
Croí a d'aithneodh creag agus caorán
Nó ceol aduain trí bhearnaí gaoithe.

Gach ball dem chuid ball a ainmníodh
De réir a chló is a chlú cheart féin –
An eisc go doimhin im chléibh,
An log sin thall, an doirín ina lár,
An tsrón, an chíoch, an lúb, an chúil,
An mhín, an cúm, an cumar, an fuarán úd

The Cailleach Speaks

for Gearóid Ó Crualaoich

Who is it I am, or what have I to relate
These days, what divining verses
To recite into the teeth of time?
What song will be sung, what tale told
From now on but the shadow of a story
A raven would tell and a grey crow deny?

    The trace of a footstep about to be sucked down
    Into the trembling moss on a bog-hole's surface.

    Lazy-beds in a reverie of sweat and banter
    Stirring themselves under forgetful bracken.

    An echo astray in the recesses of the mind
    Like an eagle's whistle in the beak of the wind.

The clay is long hidden under heather
With no trace of foot or hand laid on it
Within a memory that barely lives.
My wise ways no longer pulse up
Through vein and sinew to heart and marrow,
To hearts that would recognise crags and moors
Or strange music pouring through gaps of wind.

Each limb of my limbs that was named
For itself and for how it was known –
The gully cutting deep in my side,
That hollow there, the oaks huddled in its centre,
The jutting nose, the breast, the curve, the back,
Tableland, corrie, ravine, the spring over there

225

Leis an nglaisín ghlé ag portaireacht
Uaidh amach thar an gcaonach caoin –
A n-ainmneacha imithe le sruth is le gaoith.

Tost gan suan isea feasta mo dhán.

With the rivulet that pipes out playing
Crystal notes across the gentle moss –
All their names lost in air and water.

Now a restless silence is what I must divine.